Books by Anne Edwards:

CHILD OF NIGHT
THE HESITANT HEART
HAUNTED SUMMER
SHADOW OF A LION
MIKLOS ALEXANDROVITCH IS MISSING
THE SURVIVORS
JUDY GARLAND: A Biography
THE INN AND US (with Stephen Citron)

THE
INN
AND
US

THE INN AND US

ANNE EDWARDS

&

STEPHEN CITRON

Random House · New York

Library of Congress Cataloging in Publication Data

Edwards, Anne, 1927–
The inn and us.
1. Edwards, Anne, 1927–   —Biography.
2. Citron, Stephen. I. Citron, Stephen, joint
author. II. Title.
PS3555.D87Z52   813'.5'4   [B]   75–40557
ISBN 0-394-49602-7
Manufactured in the United States of America
2   4   6   8   9   7   5   3
First Edition

THIS BOOK IS DEDICATED
TO ALL THE
HOLIDAY INNS,
WITHOUT WHICH THERE WOULD
NEVER HAVE BEEN A NEED FOR
ORPHEUS ASCENDING

PART
ONE

I've taught American jazz in India and Siam, accompanied Piaf, composed musical scores, maintained a Carnegie Hall piano studio and played nightly in New York gin mills and Parisian boîtes, living always in a big-city, nighttime world. Why then should such a man become suddenly possessed by the desperate need to own a country inn? Insanity!

Yet . . . I had spent a part of the summer of 1970 in the small town of Stockbridge, located in the Berkshire Hills of Massachusetts. I had watched my three-year-old son run free in wildly green fields, his laughter not consumed by the screech of sirens and the squawk of horns that permeate Central Park. And I didn't have to stumble over the empty beer cans and garbage that litter the footpaths of that once glorious greenwood. The tension between my wife and me appeared eased in the presence of trees and clean streets and in the absence of the three locks on our apartment door.

Nor did the idea seem so crazy when I remembered lying under the sky on the lawn of Tanglewood, summer home of the Boston Symphony, listening to a Rachmaninoff adagio. Nor when I recalled how, remarkably, although thousands of people had been present, no one had talked. And as the concert neared its end, not a person left before the music was over.

I explained all this to Mary Pelke, the Berkshire real estate agent I had singled out to find me a suitable location for an inn, adding, "It has to be perfect, Mary. A supper club–inn, where New Yorkers and Bostonians can get away from the city and still find good music, good food and a special ambiance."

I told her about a small, elegant boîte called Le Club de Paris near the Rond-Point in Paris, where, as a young musician, I had my first professional job playing Porter, Rodgers and Hart and Gershwin to a late after-theater and dinner clientele bunched together in the intimate supper room, dining by candlelight while tuxedoed waiters hovered over them. "That's my dream, Mary—Le Club de Paris—but hours away from the crime, crush and punishment of a big city."

Mary was not too encouraging, but she didn't laugh at me either. "I'll see what there is," she replied with a small sigh. Then one gray, bleak wintry New York morning, I was half an hour late getting to Carnegie Hall because there had been no taxis on Riverside Drive. Arriving there I found the elevators kaput, delaying me further from reaching my studio. The telephone rang insistently as I fumbled with my keys. Mary was on the line.

"There's a place up for sale which, rather against my will, I feel I must tell you about," she began.

"What do you mean, 'against your will'?" I inquired.

"Well, to begin with, the place has a *long* history. It's *very* old," she underscored her words.

"How old?"

"It was built in 1847. I haven't seen it recently, but I understand it needs a lot of work, and . . . there's talk that it's haunted."

"Haunted?" I laughed.

"The ghost of an Indian princess is supposed to roam the house."

"American or Indian Indian?"

"All right, if that doesn't frighten you, it also has a more recent checkered history. The place started as a roadhouse and has been listed as a gay bar."

4

"Does it have a liquor license?" I asked.

"Yes."

"Is it transferable?"

"Yes."

"And does it have a room large enough for a piano and tables?"

"Yes."

"Tell me more."

"Well—there's a swimming pool, but I understand it's cracked on the bottom; lots of rooms, but I hear they all need a tremendous amount of work; and five acres of land directly on Route Seven. I pass there every day, Steve. No one has tended the grounds in years."

"What's the kitchen like?"

"Old. Big."

"How big?"

"I guess you could put in your piano and pipe the music through the rest of the house."

"I'll cancel my lessons and drive right up," I announced. I had immediate visions of a huge country kitchen filled with the aroma of loaves of fresh-baked French bread and steaming platters of escargots with sizzling garlic butter, with jugs of cooking wines and exotic French savories lining the top of the stove. I would bring the Berkshires what they lacked—the Gallic touch.

"Could I ask you to do me a favor before you come?" Mary Pelke asked.

"Sure, what is it?"

"Would you stop at Zabar's delicatessen and pick up a pound of hot pastrami and a loaf of Jewish rye?"

By noon I was on my way. There was a traffic tie-up on the West Side Highway, and it took me forty-five minutes to reach the first toll booth. Distracted, thinking about the inn, I pulled into the exact-change lane. "You need change. It's that line there, buddy," the toll collector shouted.

"Yeah, but I'm here and there are sixteen cars behind me!" I shouted back.

"Pull to the side!" he screamed.

Horns were blaring. The driver in the car behind me in line got out and began pounding on my closed window. "Get moving," he snarled.

I rolled down the window, almost sandpapering the tip of his nose. "I haven't got change," I snapped, and I fanned my dollar bill in his face. He grabbed it and gave me a quarter. "Hey," I complained, but he was already back in his car. For a moment I wavered, thinking I might get out of the car, drag him from his and punch him smack in the teeth. Then I remembered that I was a musician whose knuckles were important to him as well as a civilized, educated man on his way to view some property in the country. "The city does this to people," I thought. "It makes the most temperate men hostile and brawling."

I tossed the quarter into the toll box, taking my seventy-five-cent loss. I drove on, concentrating on memories of my early days as a student at the Conservatoire in Paris, recalling most vividly my room on the Rue de Douai, halfway between Clichy, where the dope peddlers hung out, and Pigalle, where the whores tramped. No. 43, two flights up, the apartment of Mignon Lombard. The furniture was rococo Louis XIV, the oval ceiling decorated with cupids and Psyche romping through painted clouds of falling plaster.

And Mignon! She was forty, looked fifty and dressed like eighteen. Her face had been ravaged by the years and was covered in tons of make-up. Her lips were always caked with an oily magenta lipstick, her eyebrows shaved and painted back on. After I had lived in her apartment for a time she confided that she shaved not only her eyebrows but all her body hair. She held that hair, except atop the head, was beastly, gauche, uncivilized and unclean. She further confessed that she shaved

6

her pubic hair and insisted that Fernand, her twenty-year-old lover, do likewise. I am not able to testify to Mignon's pubic hair, but Fernand and I once went to a public bath (when the water had been turned off because Mignon was broke), and he was, indeed, as hairless as a doorknob.

In order to supplement the money for my room and board I did household chores. Once a week I vacuumed with a machine held together with Scotch tape. To operate it required two hands on the shaft. Nothing was ever repaired. If a sofa leg collapsed, books were used to return it to its proper height. Objets d'art were turned to the wall so their broken side didn't show, since repairing anything affirmed it had been broken, while ignoring it meant it was still as it had been in *La Belle Époque*.

My favorite chores in that household centered around the cuisine. In Trenton, New Jersey, where I'd lived before coming to Paris, I had never even fried an egg. Mignon put an end to that. Helping her in the kitchen was like discovering the mysteries of centuries.

That's how I saw my own role at *my inn*. A gourmet guru bringing to my hungry, tired masses new knowledge, delights and musical joys. I would serve Mignon's steak flambée, use her recipe for pâté de campagne.

The sky was darkening ominously as I drove through the town of Great Barrington and headed onto Route 7. Stockbridge lay ten miles ahead, but the highway looked unfamiliar in the winter. The trees were bare, the roads deserted, the antique shops boarded up.

Mary was at her office when I arrived. "Ummmm! Smell that hot pastrami!" she said in ecstasy, when I handed her the bag from Zabar's.

"Smell that fresh air," I replied.

The property we had come to see was heavily forested with

evergreens. The house—a large white clapboard with yellow shutters and a full-width screened verandah—was set far back from Route 7 on the crest of a hill.

A slightly askew sign was nailed to the oak tree at the foot of the snow-covered driveway. It read:

Ye Olde Christmas Tree Inne
Selected Guests

Underneath was scrawled:

Closed for the season

" 'Selected guests.' What does that mean?" I asked.

"Well, in New England you can't just put up a sign that says Ye Olde Whore House," she explained.

I nodded in agreement.

We drove up the steep, rutted driveway. My first close view of the house revealed a sway-backed roof and broken shutters, hung at odd angles. Yet the place had an old-world elegance. It was a big, white, graceful *grande dame* of a frame building.

"La Belle Époque, almost," I thought. But I said nothing.

We parked near a dying apple tree on the edge of the thick backwoods. "What is that god-awful smell?" I asked.

"Probably the septic tank. I'm sure it hasn't been emptied in years," Mary apologized, as she rushed me to the rear door.

In a moment we were in a big dish-washing kitchen. Moldy food made the stench here worse than outside. The roaches could have put an ancient New York apartment to shame. The half-consumed food on the plates made me think of people who had eaten and run from some holocaust like Pompeii, and I expected to see their fossilized remains in the other rooms. Down a step from that room and through a narrow passageway was the main kitchen, dominated by a mammoth old black stove. I stood there marveling at it, as though I had just come upon Michelangelo's "David."

8

"It's old, of course," Mary stammered, "but look at the width of those ovens."

"It's magnificent," I added in awe.

Flanking the stove were two of the biggest refrigerators I had ever seen. Before Mary could say, "Don't!" I made the mistake of opening one. It had been turned off, and food had been left in it for what smelled like a decade. I closed the door quickly and staggered through a swinging door that was off its hinges into what must have been the bar. A few bottles of cheap wine remained on the sagging bookshelves. The smell was different here. Dead booze.

We moved on to the lounge. The floors squeaked and pitched and the ceilings were low, but there was a large brick fireplace with a huge mantel and, along one wall, windows looked out across the driveway to the front lawn and its stately border of poplars. The room was filled with old tables and chairs that even my frugal grandmother would have discarded, and as we walked across the floor, the movement sent them shimmying toward the center of the room.

"The floor may need to be jacked up. It happens in all these old houses. But this is worse than most," Mary said, shaking her head sadly. "Listen, Steve, I think this has been a mistake and I apologize . . ."

A moan came from upstairs. Mary took my hand, and as I moved in the direction of the sound, the floor creaked louder. Ghosts were one thing, but waiters having to cross that floor to serve while I sang would be something else. "No drinks will be served while Mr. Citron performs," I thought.

I pulled Mary with me as we went from the lounge to a smaller one beyond. "They called this the breakfast room," Mary explained. This didn't make sense because it was quite a distance from the kitchen. That room was connected to a sitting room about the same size in which there was a second fireplace and two large floor-to-ceiling windows, now almost entirely covered by outside foliage.

9

"Maybe you should take a room at the Red Lion Inn and come back in the morning," Mary suggested.

The day was waning, and the electricity had been turned off, but with Mary's flashlight in my hand, I headed out into the hallway to the foot of a staircase facing the door that led to a sagging verandah.

"Goodness," Mary wailed, "that looks like it has to be jacked up too."

I started up the groaning stairs. The once grand banister now had missing dowels, like a dowager who had lost a few teeth. The plaster on the ceiling threatened to fall. "Shades of Mignon Lombard," I thought.

On the second floor, they had managed to squeeze in twelve rooms, most of them partitioned cubicles suitable only for a monastery.

"They're rather tiny, aren't they?" Mary asked, following closely on my heels. "And not too private," she added. There were at least six inches of space between the top of the door and the jamb.

The moan was now directly above us. I headed up to the third floor, cracking my head on the low ceiling. Here, under the eaves, separated by a bath containing an old tub on legs, were two big rooms.

All was silence. I turned back to rejoin Mary, again cracking my head and swearing louder on the way down than I had on the way up. "The old girl stopped moaning once she knew I had seen the whole place," I said.

"There is still the basement," Mary reminded me as we returned to the lounge on the ground floor.

"Another time."

"You're not interested then? I am sorry you came all the way up, Steve, but as I said on the telephone—"

"I'm interested," I interrupted.

"You're not!"

"I am."

10

"Look, Steve, now that I have seen what a state it's in, I am not going to show it again until—"

"What's the rock-bottom price?"

"Forty-five thousand, but it needs at least twenty thousand more in renovation."

The beam of the flashlight cast a luminous circle around us, and for a moment even in that weak light, it was like standing under a stage klieg—the dust, the decay, the disrepair of the lounge vanished. I could hear laughter, tinkling glasses and applause.

"I'm going to write you a check for a thousand dollars as a deposit," I said.

Mary placed her hand on my arm. "I won't cash it. I want you to go back to New York and think hard on it. It's an old, decrepit inn, not the Blue Angel."

"Nor Le Club de Paris," I said, "but it could be. You know, the biggest celebrities used to come there—and why? Because they could dine elegantly, as late as they wanted, on marvelous food. I didn't sit down at the piano until eleven-thirty, and the last customers left at dawn."

Mary stared at me as if I were hallucinating.

"And they came because as Rita stepped through the velvet curtains I played 'You Were Never Lovelier,' and she knew she had never been; and the Club always kept Ingrid's favorite champagne on ice. Ava Gardner would sweep her Balmain dress through the gritty hallway to get to the Club's entrance-way. It was the ambiance, the sense of belonging, once inside, that mattered. That's what I'll re-create here. And besides . . ."

Mary stopped me. "Steve, do you know when the Red Lion serves most of its dinners?" I shook my head. "At six-thirty. Nobody is awake in Stockbridge at five in the morning unless they're going out to milk the cow. You're talking about a Parisian supper club—not a New England country inn."

"They'll come to my club, you'll see, even if they have to take a nap in the afternoon."

11

I sat on one of the rickety wood chairs to write my check, and as I wrote I thought: "Wait till she sees it when I'm through. So what if I have to jack up the floors and tear out a few walls to make the bedrooms larger? The lounge is going to be perfect."

Mary left, obviously convinced I was mad. And as I drove away I thought that only I could have found the ghost of an Indian princess who, like Circe, was luring me toward my fate.

I turned the rented Maverick from the side road into the cloverleaf that leads onto the Taconic Parkway. My tuxedo was hanging from the hook in the back of the car. I'd be back in time to change my clothes and be ready for the late evening sets. From now until I raised the money to open my own place, I would play just what the customers requested and, more important, just how *they* wanted it.

As I sped along I thought of how many times, by being perverse, I had lost good tips. Only the night before an old gent had come in with a young girl and requested "September Song." As I started to play it romantically, he gave me a big Polident smile and moved his balding head about two inches from the girl's nose. Out of the corner of my eye, I could see him playing kneesies—two martinis stacked up for her—ready for action. I decided to jump the plank. I shifted gears. Wham! Into the improvisation, abandoning the melody, moving into hard, driving up-tempo jazz—loud, dissonant, drowning out all the other sound, willing the lights down, the audience captive. That old "listen to me" impulse had emerged, and I enjoyed watching the effect my new rhythms had created, shattering the "moonlight and roses" mood.

The man's face turned red as he pulled away from his Lolita, and I could see that he was complaining to her about me. She had to turn around to see me (that type never lets the girl face the piano player). Then he stood up and stalked over to me.

"Hey, that's not the way to play 'September Song.' It's a romantic ballad!"

I wanted to shout anything to let him know that I might be a piano player but I was no player piano. What I wanted to say was, "If you're so fuckin' sure of how it should be played, why don't you take over yourself?" Instead, I segued into a slow tempo with cello-range melody notes while my right hand did enough arpeggios to choke a horse. He went back to his seat, but I could see that the five-dollar tip he would normally have handed me was gone with the mood.

When I returned from Stockbridge that night, the club was packed, the noise overwhelming. As I went through the evening, I took my joy from playing louder and faster. Well, the boss would love that. I recalled reading about an experiment that had been done with chickens. Canned music was piped into the coop. When slow ballads were played for the hens, they produced their normal quota of eggs. But when up-tempo tunes were piped in, damned if those hens didn't lay more eggs!

The same principle always worked in the club. Pull the strings faster and they drank faster. Play louder and they felt they were in a swinging place. It's hard for the chichi set to feel they're having a good time unless they're shouting over the music.

In that New York club, I was far from Stockbridge, but somehow I would raise the money I needed to return. And when I did it would be to *my* club in *my* inn. Then I would play only the songs I wanted, just how I felt they should be played.

Raising the money to finance a dream is not an easy matter. It had been difficult enough to convince my wife that my dream could encompass and provide for the three of us. She was a sculptor, and as an inducement I offered her a large area opposite the lounge for a gallery, as well as a section off the back kitchen for the proper studio she lacked in New York. I reminded her how good it would be for our son, Lex, to attend a school without fear of being mugged; how he could learn to play soccer on grass instead of asphalt and breathe in unpolluted air. As a clincher I added, "And it could just save him from being the son of divorced parents." She agreed.

Try as I did to get the price of the inn below $45,000, I could not. I told Mary that in her negotiations she should stress the squeaking floors, the sinking foundation, the neglected grounds. "Forty-five thousand was rock bottom," came back the reply. The highest mortgage I was able to raise from the bank was $25,000. Mary went back to the owner, who then offered a second mortgage of $10,000. That meant that an additional $10,000 was needed to complete the sale, and as Mary had indeed warned—at least $20,000 to refurbish and renovate the premises. I didn't have it.

The premises—they were a living thing now, part of my life. They had to have a name and finding one became a round-the-clock obsession. Discarded were Le Petit Musée, New York North, and Chez Steve. I remembered the Olympian feeling I had when I saw the place first and decided on "Orpheus" in homage to the spirit of music. But something was missing. Then I recalled the ride up the steep front driveway and Mary telling me that the house was on the highest elevation in Stockbridge. I hit on "Orpheus Ascending."

As it turned out, the name was a mixed blessing. The more conservative townsfolk thought it outlandish. Some were sure we cooked Greek food; no telephone operator could pronounce, spell or remember the name correctly; and during our first season a dowager leaning on a cane came in and asked in a shaky voice, "Young man, is this Oedipus Extending?"

But the name seemed just right for the brochure I wrote to send to possible investors. "Orpheus Ascending," the pamphlet began, "is to be a French country inn, a sophisticated home away from home in the beautiful Berkshires only three miles from Tanglewood, the summer residence of the Boston Symphony Orchestra. Imagine waking to bird calls and fresh orange juice and homemade croissants. Our guests will dine in the French style while listening to the songs of Cole Porter and Michel Legrand."

It took time to raise the money, but before the contracts were signed there was enough response for us to form a corporation. My family and I moved to Stockbridge to our new home. It was spring and I had thought the sun would sweep away the roaches, heal the falling plaster and seal the crevice in the bottom of the swimming pool. I was wrong. Orpheus Ascending, enthroned on the highest elevation in Stockbridge, was a ruin with a view.

The snow was late in thawing. An April blizzard had seen to that. I had expected to see green covering my five acres in the spring. There was nothing but patches of dirty snow and mud, and scattered everywhere—sometimes half-buried in the silt—garden tools rusted and unusable. I found the grave of my Indian princess beneath the farthest apple tree, a strange runic legend on her headstone: she had died of a broken heart. My first decision as a landowner was to have the princess's remains moved to the Indian burial ground on the other side of town, but all that was found when the grave was uncovered were the bones of a small dog.

The next job was to jack up the house. Metal supports had to be placed in the basement and gradually screwed up against the crossbeams. It was a huge task, and there were moments when it seemed the entire building would collapse before the support columns could be implanted. The job cost $4,000, but I smiled as I signed the check, for it was the first bill I paid on the Orpheus Ascending business-account checks.

A clean-up crew was hired for the grounds. Dead trees had to be cut down before they fell and crashed on the roof. And there were several small outbuildings—a shed, a garage, a greenhouse—that had to come down as well. Cost: $1,570.

15

The snow finally melted, and as it did, water rushed into the basement damaging the refrigerator motors. Cost of replacement: $900.

Reconstruction was initiated on the ground floor for the gallery. This meant tearing out a bathroom and turning the space into an art-storage closet and taking down a wall between two smaller rooms. Then the area had to be carpeted and spotlit. Cost: $2,200.

It rained during the entire month of May, and all exterior work had to be halted. The "season" was drawing closer— "season" means the eight weeks of the Boston Symphony's Tanglewood concerts, this year starting June 28. The merchants of Stockbridge and neighboring Lenox support themselves for the entire year from the tourists who come to the summer concerts. Time was paramount. June was upon us. The rains finally stopped. I walked my five acres to survey the damage.

The pool was a disaster. Since it was at the back of the house, and beautifully set into a ledge of Rattlesnake Mountain, it collected all the water that drained down the mountain. The water in the pool was murky brown, seemingly bottomless and alive with hundreds of croaking frogs. I considered adding frogs' legs to the menu, but since I had no idea how to catch frogs, and no heart to kill them if I found someone else who could, I quickly discarded the plan. I had a pump hooked up to the pool to get rid of the foul water, but as the water level descended, the crack in the bottom began to look like the San Andreas fault.

In desperation I called in a pool service company, feigning calm when the salesman quoted a price of $2,000 to get the pool ready. The pumps and filters had rotted, and it would be a big job. "Can you start tomorrow?" I asked, my cash reserve dwindling with every croak of those damned frogs!

That next afternoon I received a visit from Chief of Police Obie. "That pool has to be fenced if you're going to use it," he said. "In fact, even if you're *not* going to use it, it has to be fenced. It's a hazard to children and animals."

The day was hot, and when he asked me for a glass of water, I had this idea that I could soft-soap him a bit. "How about some iced tea?" I offered, and when he nodded, I brought him into the kitchen. He looked around, eyebrows raised.

"You intend to serve food from this kitchen?" he scoffed. "Where's the exhaust fan? You can't use wood drainboards, and where's your emergency exit?"

"Well, we haven't got it together yet," I explained, "we've been working on the gallery."

"When you do get it together, you'll have to notify the board of health," he warned. "They have to approve it before you can sell even a glass of beer."

I sat down on one of the benches outside the bar door after I had shown Obie out. "Why am I here?" I asked myself.

I heard the sound of childish laughter. Lex was playing alone on the front lawn chasing a rabbit. There was the sweet smell of lilacs in the air and the sky was a deep blue. The light was incredibly sharp, and the near bushes, the clumps of wild flowers, the evergreens and poplars, were all crisply defined like notes from a master pianist. In the city, summer was blurred and the heat only intensified the stench of the refuse. I breathed deeply. There were soft breezes here, the smell of freshly mown grass and the pungent aroma of the evergreen nearest the porch. As a child I had only cement beneath my feet and telephone poles and wires above my head where oaken trunks and shady branches might have been. There had been no more than twenty feet between my bedroom window and the house next door.

A delivery truck turned up the driveway. That's my road, I boasted to myself. It took several minutes for it to make the full length, circle the center roundabout and pull in back by the kitchen. "My land," I said out loud.

That was part of it: being a landowner.

17

"Where's the boss?" I heard the deliveryman ask.

That was another part of it. But there was more, much more. Teaching music had always meant a great deal to me. I had taught all kinds—classical, popular, voice, composition—but the most personally gratifying experience had always been to teach someone to really listen to a melody, to sing it, then to pick it out on the piano and later to find for himself the chords that go with the tune. That is self-accompaniment by ear. What a joy it was when I could then teach my students their first chord—C—a chord which represents peace, completion . . . home.

I would be away from my students for the ten weeks of the summer season, but for the first time in my life I felt that I myself had found the first chord. I thought I was home.

"You Mr. Citron?" the red-faced uniformed driver asked.

"Yes, I am."

"I need a check for eight hundred and ninety-two dollars and fifty-four cents. Bill says collect on delivery. It's for wood siding and roof shingles."

Home.

The next day the pool man returned. "If you're gonna use this pool, Mr. Citron, my first estimate was too low. You'll have to drill for water. It will never work on the spring," he confided.

Twenty thousand dollars was not going to cover the reconstruction, the renovations, the opening expenses *and* a pool. Most of it was gone already. "How much more will that cost?" I asked.

"Depends on how deep we have to go, and if we run into rock," he said glumly. "And who knows what other problems we'll find."

"It will have to wait until next summer, I'm afraid. But I'll go over my books and let you know for sure."

One glance at my bank balance later that day convinced me that I would indeed have to abandon the pool for the summer and put top priority on satisfying the board of health.

18

The reality facing me was that my cash was already down to nil. I had been undercapitalized at $20,000. It seemed appalling to go back to my investors before the doors of Orpheus were even open. I went to the bank bright and early the next morning, applied for a home improvement loan and, thankfully, got it. Work then commenced on the kitchen. Sinks were repaired, floors covered, fans screened, the remarkable old black Garland stove hooded and an emergency exit door cut into the kitchen wall.

June 15 was set as opening night, a trial run before the big Tanglewood rush. The menu was to be simple. I could make a big batch of Mignon Lombard's pâté, prepare dozens of escargots which the waiter could simply place under the broiler, precook a huge kettle of onion soup gratinée that could be poured into serving crocks and refrigerated, and prepare a cold gazpacho that would need only to be spooned into iced bowls. Entrées would be crêpes stuffed with either shrimp or chicken, cooked, frozen and ready for the final steps, and I, myself, would prepare filet mignon flambée, *sur commande*, between sets. I figured I could start the steak, emerge from the kitchen and play Cole Porter's "It's All Right with Me," giving two choruses for a rare filet, three for medium and four for well done. I would have a built-in musical timer.

As the work load increased, so did the problems between my wife and me. Never before had there been a need for a power struggle in our relationship. Previously she had her work and home and I had my work and my music. The marriage was shaky but had survived six years because we were each involved in separate pursuits. Now life became a daily battle of pronouns. A war of priorities was raging between *our* gallery and *our* inn. I soon realized it was *her* gallery and *my* inn. If I was nearing the fulfillment of a dream, I was also close to losing a wife.

It was already June, though, and I could not afford to ponder this. If we didn't open for the season we were in danger of losing both her gallery *and* my inn. Yet the closer we got to June 28, the more unlikely it seemed that we would be ready. What we needed was more help to get the place in shape, but the salaries of professionals were prohibitive. I weighed the revenues the third floor would bring if used for guest rooms against how much I could save by using it for dormitory rooms for city teenagers who might want to spend the summer in the country and earn tips as well. I made calls to friends and agencies in New York. Three young men and two eager girls soon signed on, and I waited expectantly for them to arrive.

In the meantime I had what local help I was able to get paint the walls of the lounge a bright shiny blue. With the red rug and white curtains and a freshly scrubbed red brick fireplace the room now had the look of the French tricolor. I carried the look outside, bordering the driveway with large, white flower tubs and planting them with red, white and blue petunias.

But I was haunted by the memory of the delicate quince blossoms in the courtyard of a country inn in the South of France where I had once stayed. I took Lex in the car with me the next day. "Where are we going, Daddy?" he asked.

"To Ward's Nursery," I replied.

"Is it like a nursery school?" he asked.

"No, they take care of all kinds of young plants."

"Then it is like my school, only for plants."

At Ward's, when I asked for a quince tree, it was explained to me that though they had a few in the greenhouse, the Berkshires were a bit too far north for quince. I said I still would like one, and the proprietor warned me that it would have less than a fifty-fifty chance of survival. "Too far north," he repeated as he shook his head.

I chose a small tree that looked healthy. A few unopened orange buds were on its fragile branches. The nursery man said he would not guarantee it.

When we got back to Orpheus, Lex and I immediately set to planting the tree on the edge of the driveway. I kept referring to it as our own quince tree, and Lex told me, with the honesty of the young, that it was just a bush.

"Will it grow to be a tree?" he asked.

"Yes, one day it will be a tall tree."

"Will I always be bigger than it—like now?"

"You'll be taller for a long time. Then one day you will stop growing and the quince will continue."

"That's no fair," he said.

We watered it for days. The leaves were sagging. Then, the stillborn buds began dropping off. I thought of what the nursery man had said. We were really too far north for quince. And no guarantee. You couldn't make things grow just because you wanted them to.

"Maybe it's too far north for me, too," I thought. And then quickly dismissed the idea.

The first of the staff to arrive was Larri. His spelling of his name on his application should have prepared me for a certain pretentiousness, but I wasn't ready for the MG that revved up our driveway that June afternoon, golf clubs sticking out of the window, three Gucci bags stowed in the trunk. He was to be our dishwasher. I walked with him to the attic dormitories and somehow I found myself carrying his bag, treating him as if he were our first guest. He was somewhat disgruntled that there were two beds in the room besides his own, but I ignored it and turned to leave so he could get on with his unpacking. He stopped me, saying, "By the way is there a good tailor in town? My dinner jacket got really crushed in the boot of the car."

"Why did you bring a dinner jacket?" I asked, puzzled.

"When I went to the Tanglewood concerts with my parents last year we always wore them."

"Well, this year your busiest time will be during the concerts." He looked crestfallen. "You'll be able to go to the open rehearsals on Saturday mornings," I added by way of compensation. "That's how all the professionals hear the music." I

21

made my way downstairs thinking, "That's just what I need, a rich kid, his first time away from home."

An hour later he emerged in newly pressed jeans. "Larri reporting for work, mon-soor." He grinned.

I led him into the back kitchen where the sinks were filled with pots and pans from the pâté and crêpes now, cooked and ready to freeze. When he complained that there wasn't a machine to do the pots, I said, "You're the machine."

I spent the rest of the morning trying to solve a construction problem. In redoing the gallery ceiling, a workman had put his axe in the wrong place and the plaster had fallen. There was now a gaping hole in the ceiling. My wife was furious. The workmen were stymied. And I was dead center of a new battle. In the midst of all this Larri appeared.

"What time is lunch served?" he asked.

"There's food in the refrigerator near the window. Make yourself a sandwich," I replied. Turning back to the problem, I decided that since a beam had been exposed, time and money would be saved by pulling down all the plaster. Then, when we exposed the beams, we would have a higher and more interesting ceiling. My wife agreed and the workmen began hacking away at the plaster.

I went into the kitchen. Larri had taken a filet, which I had bought at forty-five cents *an ounce* to test Annie's recipe, cut it in half and grilled it. "Is it all right that I made two sandwiches?" he asked. "The meat was too thick to fit on one."

The first girl arrived that afternoon, dropped off at the house by her brother, who thanked me profusely for "taking the girl in." Their mother had died recently, and Laura, who was "shy," would really appreciate a summer in the country. He thought it would help her to "come out of herself." While he was talking, Laura sat in the car, and when her brother carried her bag up to the third floor, I had a little talk with her. Rather, I talked and Laura nodded her head. With shoulder-length hair

22

and granny glasses, and dressed in a muumuu of some gauzy material, she looked like a wraith and kept her head bowed all the time. After finding out that she could indeed make a bed and clean a room (she was to be our chambermaid), I commented on her muumuu, and she told me she had made it. I set her to work cutting and hemming a bolt of cloth into bedspreads. Later, when I remarked that some of her seams were zigzagged, she dissolved into tears, ran to the third floor and did not appear for dinner or breakfast.

The other young people duly arrived. The girl who was to be our waitress appeared for a run-through of her duties in a diaphanous orange chiffon gown; our bartender had only had a three-day crash course at a bartending school; and our handyman, Doug, turned out to be a health and nature freak who gave everyone lectures on the moral and physical dangers of consuming meat. At mealtimes he treated us as though we were guilty of the worst aberration known to mankind.

Those last few days before our "Pre-Grand Opening" were madness and bedlam, but finally the carpet was laid, a black slab of marble installed as a bartop, Carnegie Hall posters affixed to the bar walls, the gallery opened, the rooms ready for occupancy, the kitchen stocked, the grounds cleaned and "Entrée" painted in blue outside the door to the bar.

That night when everyone had gone to bed, I picked up the local newspaper and there it was—our big announcement:

OPENING TOMORROW
ORPHEUS ASCENDING
The Berkshires' only Chansonier . . .
Diner—Souper—Jusqu'à Minuit

My mind was racing. Had I put too much salt in the pâté? Had I bought enough filets? What if we ran out of something? What if nobody came? Was there a supply of propane gas for

23

the oven? Were four brands of gin enough? And why the hell hadn't my tuxedo come back from the cleaners?

I went into the bar and turned on the muted pink-orange lights. We had at least achieved atmosphere. I poured myself a double Scotch and sat on one of the tall black leather chairs. What was I trying to create after all? Why did I need all the extra work, the new debts, the additional worries that opening an inn–cum–supper club presented?

Drink a lot and you're bound to get maudlin. I had a bar stocked with the best Scotch. As I drank and dug into my true motives, I began to understand that my shaky marriage, as much as my need to leave the city, had driven me to Stockbridge. Further, my wife never would have joined me in this venture if I hadn't bribed her with the promise of her own gallery. Hadn't I batted out in a previous marriage? Hadn't I screwed around in both? Maybe I wasn't capable of real loving. Maybe I demanded—unfairly—that I be loved only on my terms.

Perhaps, I finally decided, this is going to be it: my mistress-wife, this ancient house with a bogus ghost and the promise of stimulating guests.

I went into the lounge and sat down at the big black Steinway. The room was dark except for the stage lights with their colored gels. I began to play and to sing. Now it wasn't an empty lounge, it was Le Club de Paris and out in that darkness there was someone—one person—who was listening and who understood.

Understood what?

Me.

I played until the dark was gone and the birds were pecking away at the feeder I had hung for them. It was opening day.

By five that evening everything was ready. Doug had connected the wires electrifying the sign out front. Bright lanterns were strung on the verandah and spotlights installed on the front lawn. We could be seen from a mile down the road in either direction. I had remembered the dictum of the owner of the last New York boîte I worked in: "If you want the people to come, light up the outside in a blaze of glory. People are drawn to light like moths to the flame. But inside let them stumble to their seats in candlelight and anonymity. They'll be amorous, drink, hold hands and drink more. Discourage the food, encourage the drinking. Charge outlandish prices. They will tell their friends about the outrageous boîte they were in and their friends will come to be outraged more."

I didn't buy the last part, but I would open Orpheus Ascending in a blaze of glory. I threw the light switch. Nothing happened. The lights were working, but so was the sun. Atmosphere in the Berkshires has to wait until 9:00 P.M. when night falls in the summer.

The waitress was in the kitchen warming the oven for the crêpes. Larri was at his dishwashing station. Laura was helping the waitress. Ken, the bartender, stood at attention behind the black marble bar, smartly red-jacketed, bow-tied and clean-shaven. My wife was begowned and at the desk in her gallery, and since my tuxedo never returned from the cleaner, I wore a striped silk shirt open at the neck—perhaps a bit daring for the Berkshires but pleasantly theatrical.

A Lincoln Continental pulled up the driveway, and I was grateful now for Larri's MG parked in a conspicuous place. I sat myself coolly at the cash register, pretending to count the contents—which I had already counted three times. The driver parked the car next to the MG and a man in a Brooks Brothers suit got out, leaving a girl sitting inside. "Probably wants to check the place out," I told the bartender. Then I shouted for the waitress. "Greet him with the menu," I ordered her. "May I help you?" she inquired, holding out a menu. "How far is the Red Lion Inn?" he asked.

I slammed the register drawer loudly. "Two miles down the road. Turn right at the foot of the driveway."

He turned and stopped. "Nice bar. Just open?"

I looked nervously to the empty lounge beyond. "We plan a big late-night business," I apologized.

"Maybe we'll see you later then." He walked to the parking lot, and as he neared the car, the girl rolled down her window. They talked briefly and then both headed back to the bar door. I rushed to the piano to play "La Vie en Rose," hoping to seduce them into staying.

The girl wanted to use the powder room.

By seven no one had shown up, so I had Doug change from his jeans and Laura dress in her muumuu to act as customers seated at a table next to my wife and me. I started a Patachou record, had the waitress prepare us crêpes, the bartender open champagne.

Finally a couple dressed in tennis clothes got out of a beat-up old Ford and came into the bar. I jumped up to greet them. He was the new chef at the Pittsfield Hilton on his day off. I served them a complimentary order of pâté. He asked for the recipe, which I eagerly gave to him to read. And he paid me with a ten-dollar bill, which I proudly taped to the bar mirror.

There was the sound of a smooth motor. The Lincoln Continental had returned.

"We found the Red Lion Inn," the man in the Brooks Brothers suit told me, "but it looked stuffy, so we brought our friends back with us."

Another car came up the driveway. Soon there were five, and I was playing the host, the *patron*, moving from table to table, overseeing the staff.

"What the hell is that?" I thought, watching horrified as the waitress served a martini straight up with a black olive instead of the standard green one. I rushed over to the table with a ready smile. "We serve our martinis with a black olive. It makes a smoother, drier drink. Hope you enjoy it."

"How chic!" His girlfriend smiled back, and I knew he would never drink a green-olived martini again.

All our energies had been directed to readying the ground floor for the pre-Tanglewood opening. To do that we had postponed work upstairs, since the guest bedrooms would not be occupied until the first Tanglewood weekend.

The next morning we all attacked the second floor in earnest, painting, stapling fabric on the walls, sewing curtains and repairing windows at a furious pace. The days were hot and sunny and we would take breaks poolside, amusing ourselves by watching the frogs splash around in the muddy water at the bottom of the tank, thinking how damned lucky they were. Everyone grew bronzed and healthy, if exhausted.

My studio was closed for the summer, and I was no longer going into the city. Our "cash reserve" was nonexistent, but the restaurant and bar were open, business had increased from our first night and, more heartening, customers were returning. Still, we had not one room reservation for the season. I called the inns in the area and lied: "We still have a few rooms left on certain weekends." They were grateful to know a local place to send their overflow and within a week bookings came in.

All the rooms were reserved for the first night of the concert season, and on Friday afternoon the houseguests began to arrive. The price of the room included only breakfast, but most of our guests had reserved tables for dinner before the concert. When one of my students, Jay Wilamowski, pressed me, I even agreed that he could stay on a cot in the large windowless linen closet, with a fan running.

Orpheus was bursting at the seams that hot, dry afternoon of June 28 when we officially opened as a complete inn. I had been taking dinner reservations by telephone, and we were up to twenty-four, in addition to our guests. I was ecstatic. Then I saw our menu which, to my horror, read:

Pate de Champagne	$1.35
Oeuf dur Mayonnaise avec Salade Russe	.85
Soup a'L'Onion gratinee	1.70
Escargots de Borgignone	
Les Six	2.10
La Douzaine	3.90
Gazpacho	.90
Crepe de Chicken	3.60*
Crepe de Shrimp	3.60*
Filet Mignon Flambe au Calvados	4.10
*Served with Small Roquefort Salad	
Salade Frais au Roquefort	2.30
Salade de Shrimp au Roquefort	2.95
Pecan Pie with Real Whipped Cream	1.15
Mousse au Chocolat	.95
Fresh Peaches in Port Wine	1.05
Blueberries avec Creme Fraiche	1.05
Cafe	.40
Thé Aromatisé	.40
(Darjeeling—English Breakfast)	
(Oriental Blend—Jasmine)	

Larri, who had claimed a fine command of written French, had been given the task of hand-printing our menus. Unfortunately I hadn't had time to correct his appalling spelling or the fact that what he was unable to translate he wrote in English. I would prepare a new menu myself the next morning.

One reservation came in for a Mrs. Barber, who wanted a table for three at 7:00 P.M., "near the piano, if the music wasn't too loud."

Stephanie Barber was a legend in Berkshire County. She sang, ran an elegant inn, held a real estate license, and was well known for her flamboyant costumes. She had previously owned Music Inn and had been responsible for bringing, among others, Billie Holiday, to the area. If she liked Orpheus it could be a start. I put a big RESERVED card on the table nearest the piano.

Only moments later I heard our one and only waitress on the pay telephone. She was apparently calling the Red Lion Inn. "Yes, I can come in tomorrow. What time? Lunch and dinner?"

I confronted her.

"There's just not enough money to be made here and I have to support myself at college through the winter," she said frankly. "I'll stay tonight and help train Laura."

"Laura!" I shouted. "Why, she'll burst into tears if someone complains about a missing fork!"

"Don't yell at me," she said.

"Yell?" I tried to control myself but could not. "You want to go to the Red Lion? Go. NOW!"

"Tonight? But where?"

"Rent a room anywhere, but get out!" I handed her twenty dollars' pay, and she broke into tears and flew up the stairs to the attic dormitory.

In my anger at the girl because she had given us no warning, I left us opening without a waitress, so I took Larri aside. "Larri," I said, patting him on the shoulder, "you are going to be the maître d'hôtel." I thought that title would please him more than the term "waiter." "You can wear your dinner jacket," I added as a further enticement.

"But I don't know anything about serving," he said.

"It's simple. You serve from the right and take away from the left. Or is it the other way around?" I asked. "No matter. There are only two things to remember. One: see that everybody has a big piece of cheese and a loaf of bread as soon as they sit down. And two: cover your inexpertise with flair." I leaned in closer. "Don't worry, Larri, you're a natural," I assured him. "And don't get nervous. I'll get Doug to do the dishes later. Where is he anyway? I need him to do something for me right away."

"Doug's up on the roof," Larri said.

"What's he doing up there?"

29

"The people in Room six noticed a wasps' nest in the corner by the window. In fact, a couple of hornets came into their room. Do the forks go to the left or the right?"

There was a crash and I ran outside. Some of the shingles and part of the support for the eaves had been knocked down along with hosts of angry wasps, but Doug, though a bit scratched and breathless, was unscathed.

"Think you could manage another job right now?" I asked him. "A branch has to be cut from the big oak. It's covering the sign at the entrance to the driveway."

"Steve, you know I'd do anything for you, but I'd sooner cut off my right arm than cut a healthy branch from that beautiful old oak," he replied.

"But we can't be seen from the road," I protested.

"Is commercialism more important than a living thing?"

"Yes."

"Well, you can fire me, but that's one thing my conscience won't allow me to do."

We stood facing each other in a battle of wills. Like a drowning man, images flashed before my eyes: pots and pans stacked to the kitchen ceiling, the sound system dead and no one to repair it. "Okay, Doug," I said, deciding to cut the branch the next day myself, "how about helping with the pots and pans, then?"

"Glad to oblige." He grinned and disappeared into the back kitchen.

At five-thirty the first houseguests came down to dinner and Larri took their orders. He seemed calm enough and looked splendid in his white jacket. I breathed a sigh of relief.

My student, Jay, came limping into the dining room. He whispered to me that since his room was so hot he had taken off all his clothes, lay down for a nap and rolled over onto a couple of wasps. One had stung him on the thigh, the other —as he put it—"further up." I commented that he was lucky he hadn't rolled over onto his front, or it might have been a disaster. He agreed nervously, adding, "The entire second floor has been invaded."

I dispatched Doug to cope with that new problem, put on a Piaf record and went in to supervise the kitchen and to help Larri serve.

The dining room was almost full. I was having my first taste of what Tanglewood means to a Berkshire restaurateur. There is no such thing as staggered dining. The concerts start at eight-thirty, and everyone has to eat and be out before eight in order to park their cars at the concert and be seated in time. Nothing in the kitchen was working as smoothly as it had on our trial run. There wasn't room under the broiler for as many escargot and onion soup gratinée orders as we were getting. I burnt one batch of French bread and Laura, trying to be helpful, had put a loaf of pâté in the oven, believing it was meat loaf, to be served hot.

The bartender popped his head through the new swinging door. "Mrs. Barber," he whispered.

I went to greet a man and two women. There was no doubt in my mind which woman was Stephanie Barber. She had been described to me once as always being costumed, never just dressed. All eyes in the room were on a regal blond lady wearing a white satin gown and carrying a black ostrich-feather fan. She smiled mysteriously at me, arched a penciled brow and introduced me to her companions in a husky Dietrich voice. "We'll have some pâté and salad," she cooed, and did we have a Cabernet-Sauvignon blanc? No, I apologized, but my pâté would be better complemented by a rosé d'Anjou. . . .

"*Très glacé, s'il vous plaît?*" said Mrs. Barber.

At that moment Larri burst through the swinging door with a large tray. His foot caught in the carpet and down went the tray. Escargots and onion soup gratinée spilled over the dining room floor. Fortunately he had missed the guests. I went into the kitchen to get Laura.

"You'll have to clean up that mess," I told her.

"I can't go out there with all those people," she cried. "I'd die." Doug said he would do it, but he was dressed in jeans. Larri was visibly shaken by the accident, so I told him to remain in the kitchen. I asked him to lend Doug his dinner jacket, and I hoped the rest of Doug's outfit would not be noticed.

I would serve the Barber party myself. I realized I had never served anyone except in my own home before and decided that was the manner I would adopt. They were guests in my home. As I went to fill Mrs. Barber's glass with wine, she touched my sleeve, *"Pas trop, pour moi.* I don't want to be *étourdie* for the concert."* As I turned to serve the man's wine, the heel of the bottle caught the rim of the glass and rosé splashed down the front of his impeccable white dinner jacket.

"We should have had white wine." Mrs. Barber laughed. "That way it wouldn't have shown."

"I'll have it cleaned, of course," I blurted, "but can I send someone to your house to get another jacket while you eat?" It wasn't good enough but it was all I could think of.

"It's all right," he said kindly, "I'll manage with this one."

"The wine is with my compliments," I offered, immediately realizing how foolish that sounded. We all laughed. "Can I make it up some way?" I asked.

"I hear you are a specialist in French chansons," Mrs. Barber said. "Would you do some for us?"

I was only too happy to sit down at the piano, and I plunged fortissimo into *"Padam . . . Padam,"* a song about a man obsessed with a melody spinning in his head. Mrs. Barber was close enough to the piano for me to see that she was mouthing the words along with me as I whirled faster and louder through the lyric. She knew the song and obviously understood that all those decibels were essential to an honest interpretation. I segued into *"Le Chevalier de Paris,"* whose lyric tells of a man caught up in the daily grind of life in the city and how he longs for his youth in the country. While I sang, I could see the bartender frantically signaling me. I cut the third chorus.

"Oh, *mon cher*," said Mrs. Barber as I left the piano. *"Formidable!* But I was hoping you would do the last verse. *C'est significatif, oui?"*

"Oui, but it also seems people want to pay their checks so that they can get to the concert," I apologized.

She followed me into the bar. "Do you also sing *'Non, je ne regrette rien'?"*

"Yes, I do."

"Any Jacques Brel?"

"Yes," I nodded, totting up checks and running American Express charges through the machine.

"But, *mon cher,"* she exclaimed, "we have the same repertoire!" She stood patiently until I had a moment free. "You've done a fine job," she complimented me. "The place is so attractive. Why, I remember when it was known only for . . . shall we say . . . ladies of the evening?"

I thanked her, and she added, "I will be back very soon." Leaning over and kissing me on the cheek, she said, "Welcome to the Berkshires, *cheri."*

It was now only ten after eight but the place had almost emptied out. A few drinkers remained at the bar and in the lounge, apparently too timid to face an all-Bach program. By nine no more cars came up the driveway. By ten—zilch.

"Okay, Citron," I thought. "That was it." I told the staff to start cleaning up, and I sat down to count the take. Over four hundred dollars. Not bad. Once the kinks were out, once the staff was trained, I could spend more time at the piano, and there would be an audience I could communicate with. Stephanie Barber had given me hope that such an audience did exist.

At about eleven o'clock, to my great surprise, some cars came up the driveway. I sat down at the piano and while I sang I was aware of the sound of motors and slamming car doors and

33

the jangling of the Indian bells over the entry. I ended my set and clicked off the spots. The lounge was filled to capacity. I went into the bar. It was jammed. Cars were parked all over the front lawn. "I hope no one drives over the quince tree," I thought.

Ken, the bartender, was struggling to keep up with the orders and looking desperately to me for help. "You're on solo, baby," I told him. "Make the most of it." Then I disappeared into the kitchen before he could protest.

I had Laura and the second chambermaid furiously preparing more escargots. The butter wouldn't soften. Laura turned the oven up high. I heard a crack. She had forgotten that the plates on which the crêpes were warming inside the oven were not ovenproof. The stove was a mess. Smoke was pouring out through the gas jets and permeated the kitchen. We were all choking. "Get some more crêpes," I ordered Laura. "There are no more!" she said. "We haven't anything left but pâté and pecan pie." I wanted to reply, "Why the fuck didn't you tell me earlier?" But I decided it wouldn't help. Tomorrow, first thing, I would hire a chef. "Close the kitchen," I shouted. "No more food served." Larri had just swung into the kitchen.

"Everyone wants to know where the fire is," he said.

"Tell them it's a special recipe for smoked pork chops that I'm preparing for tomorrow night, and if they'll come back then they're in for a fantastic eating experience. In the meantime, Larri, like I said—no more food. Push the drinks. Unless someone wants pâté and pecan pie with real whipped cream."

"Pâté and pecan pie?" he said, looking ill.

"No comments, just push the booze."

At the bar Ken was in a further panic. We were almost out of ice.

"One cube per drink," I whispered to him. "Tell them you're English. Tell them anything. In the meantime I'll send Doug out for more ice."

I went into the back kitchen. "Where's Doug?" I asked Laura.

"In the woodshed."

"What's he doing there?"

"Room four wanted a bedboard. The man has a bad back."

I stopped Doug as he came around the corner of the woodshed rolling an old round table top toward the back stairway. "Leave that for now and get some ice," I told him.

The night was clear and the moon nearly full. There was a soft breeze and out there by the woodshed, next to the swimming pool, all I could hear were croaking frogs. I had wanted an inn and I had wanted the country. Maybe this is what happened when you wished for too much. A round table top for a single bed and a muddy pool of croaking frogs!

When I came back into the kitchen Ken was frying himself some eggs. "I just can't cope with that many people," he explained.

"Who's tending bar?"

"Nobody."

I took several pads of checks, ran into the bar and announced, "Ladies and gentlemen, our bartender is ill. I invite you to make your own drinks—go easy on the ice until we get fresh supplies. Write down what you've had on these pads and put your names on the top."

Everyone loved the idea. None of them had ever had the chance to step behind a professional bar before, and I realized a lot of people were frustrated bartenders.

At the height of all this conviviality, four half-polluted men stumbled in. One asked me where Nellie was.

"Nellie who?" I asked.

"You know," he said, poking me in the ribs with his elbow, "the one with the b-i-i-g . . ." and he made the usual gesture.

"Well," I told him, "we've changed the policy."

"Yeah, I see. Looks like you're going in for guys now," he

said eyeing all the men who were making drinks for their dates in the lounge.

"No, it's mixed couples. Everything's quite straight."

He looked around.

"Lemme have a Schlitz," the first guy said.

"We only serve Heineken's and Wurtzberger."

"Wass wrong with American beer?"

"Nothing, only . . ." Then I had an idea. "Nellie? Nellie. Oh, I know the Nellie you mean. She works over at the Hearthstone Inn off Route forty-one in Housatonic." I had pulled the place out of my imagination and purposely situated it in the most godforsaken spot I could think of.

As they shuffled to the door I shouted, "You'd better hurry. I think she's off at half past twelve."

"You're a real sport," one guy yelled back as they poured out the door and piled into their car.

We closed the bar at one. Shortly after that, Doug returned with the ice.

"I had to swipe it from the Holiday Inn," he confessed.

"It's too late, but put it in the freezer. We'll probably need it tomorrow night." I sent everyone to bed and then went out to inspect the little quince tree. It was unharmed. I toured through the house. There were piles of unwashed dishes on every counter of the kitchen. I straightened what I could and sat down to make a list of what I had to do in the morning.

Cut branch from oak tree
Get second dishwasher and a waiter
Fire Ken
Make tons of food
Hire chef

Early next morning I cut the branch from the old oak tree while Doug stood there, begging me to raise the sign above the offending branch. I explained that the following year I would

36

only have to raise it again. "Would you cut off someone's leg if he was blocking your view?" he asked angrily. "No. I'd ask him to move, but I can't do that with an oak tree." With that I whacked off the branch.

Next, I called applicants I hadn't hired and found another dishwasher and waiter. I chose as cook a bright, genial girl named Rebecca and gave her my recipes. She proved to be a natural.

But I couldn't fire Ken. Anyone could have a lapse, I figured. He was just a young, inexperienced kid.

By nightfall we had sufficient ice, liquor and food. During the quiet of the concert hours everything was cleaned and set up for the late crowd. This time when the throngs began pouring in, I was prepared. Doug had even put a pile of stones around the quince tree. As I started my late-night set I was feeling secure and happy, too happy for sad songs, so I switched to a glib Cole Porter group.

The Canadian gentleman in Room 5 was at my elbow. "Hey, Citron," he said, "there's no water." He was leaning in too close for me to ignore him, so I drew the set to a close.

"I'll get Laura to fill a carafe for you to take to your room," I told him.

"I don't mean drinking water. When you turn on the tap, there's nothing," he explained.

"I'll look after it right away," I assured him, and quickly disappeared into the kitchen and opened the taps. A trickle of sandy water—then *nothing*. My stomach churned. I remembered the warnings from Mary and the pool man that the spring might not provide enough water. Doug was at my side.

"There was too little rain in June to fill the cistern by the spring, I guess," he suggested.

Things kept ticking off in my head. There was club soda and wine to drink. But cooking? And dishes? And the toilets? I remembered how Mignon Lombard used to flush the john with wine when the water bill was unpaid. "Get some pitchers of

soda, fill the tanks and leave a pitcher on every tank top," I
ordered Doug. That would work until we ran out of soda. I
went out to look at the sky. Cloudless, no rain in sight. I
returned to the lounge and distractedly played another set.
Then I got Doug, and flashlights in hand, we went to locate
the cistern in the backwoods, thinking it might be blocked and
we could somehow unblock it. We lifted the top and shone the
light down. Mud.

Colonel Wilde, who sold us our milk, owned the big dairy
farm across the road. In total desperation I called and asked if
he could give me enough water to get us through Sunday, when
most of our guests would be checking out. "Too late now," he
said, "but come over first thing in the morning. I'm always up
at dawn with the cows."

So was I.

I saw the Colonel standing in a strawberry patch near his
farmhouse. He was a tall, lean old gentleman who looked
weathered and straight in the dawn light coming over his
shoulder and across his fields.

I had spent a sleepless night worrying. How would I appease
my guests if this didn't work? How was I ever going to run an
inn without water? "What will I do?" I said as I got out of my
battered convertible and crossed to him, wringing my hands
and somehow believing for a moment that my father was
standing there.

He shifted weight and cleared his throat. "Have a strawberry, Mr. Citron," he said. "If you don't calm down you will
only make yourself sick."

When my mother died I could not cry, and I recall someone
asking me later, "What could have made you cry then?" I had
replied, "The sound of a C-major chord." But as I looked at
that old man's outstretched hand filled with strawberries, I
cried. I couldn't stop the flow of tears, and strangely I didn't
feel embarrassed. The Colonel just turned away, as though he
dealt every day with the tears of middle-aged men. He went

into his barn, emerging a minute later with two of his milkmen. "These chaps will fill enough forty-gallon milk cans to get you through," he said. "We'll bring them over in the milk truck."

I got behind the wheel of my car. "What can I do to thank you?" I managed.

"Well," he said slowly, "you could invite me over for dinner."

By the time I arrived back at the inn, the guests were down for breakfast. The coffee they drank was slightly bubbly, having been made with club soda, but they were all sympathetic to my dilemma and told me not to concern myself with them. Laura was heating pots of club soda for washing the essentials, but for some reason, the staff had switched to Bitter Lemon for the toilets.

Doug suggested a dowser who would know where to drill for water, and the man came within an hour, carrying what looked like a giant wooden wishbone. As he walked slowly around the grounds, Doug and I followed silently in his footsteps, pausing wherever he did. He would mumble to himself, and I would lean in closer to catch his words, hoping he had found the spot. But then he would move on with no comment except a shake of his head. About five hundred yards from the house he fell down on his knees. "Yippee!" he shouted, sounding like a forty-niner who had just struck gold. Then he jumped to his feet and patted me on the shoulder. "Mr. Citron, you have water," he proclaimed. "No more than fifty feet down, I'd say."

The dowser planted a big stake in the ground and then walked back to the house to collect his fifty-dollar check.

"You're sure there's water there?" I asked, as he prepared to leave.

"Well, there's no guarantee, but I'd dig there if I were you."

He had just left when Colonel Wilde called. In his clear voice, he said, "It seems to me that when the Ripleys had that place, years and years ago, there was a well that they used. I remembered it after you left. Could still be there. You better check that out. Cheaper than drilling for a new one."

I sent Doug out immediately on a search for anything vaguely resembling an abandoned well. A long time later, he burst excitedly into the house. "I found the old well near the pool pump," he said breathlessly. "It was covered with a board, and there were lots of leaves on top."

I thought about that old magic man with my fifty bucks, but I wasted no time in worrying about the lost money. I called a well-drilling company and explained my predicament. Yes, it was Sunday, but the owner could come over with his crew if I was willing to pay double time.

By early afternoon they had arrived and in less than two hours announced that they had struck water in the old well. By four the pipes had been connected. Hanson, the boss, came into the kitchen and with a dramatic gesture that made it look like he was causing water to flow from limestone, turned on the tap. The water gushed out. I reached for a glass, but his large, muddied hand restrained me.

"I wouldn't do that if I were you," he said. "That well is right squat next to what used to be the outhouse. There's a damned good chance it's polluted. You can use it for flushing toilets but not for drinking, cooking or washing dishes until the lab checks it out."

"What happens if it's no good?" I asked.

"Guess we'll have to drill another well someplace else on the property." He wiped his brow and put on his hat. "I'll drop a sample over to the lab by tomorrow. You should get their answer by Tuesday."

"By Tuesday!" I shouted, knowing that in three days I'd be dead of anxiety. "How did the other owners manage?"

"Heard they didn't wash much. Used a lot of cologne though." He accented the next words, *"I heard."*

"How much is this going to cost me?" I asked apprehensively as he was leaving.

"Well, course I can't be accurate yet, but with a new pump and all I figure something like twenty-four hundred."

I told the staff that we could not open for dinner until the water problem was solved, and I went down to the road to hang the CLOSED sign. I might have been carrying my own tombstone. The weekend guests were all leaving, and the Canadian waved to me as he passed, turning onto the highway in the direction of the Red Lion Inn, I glumly noted.

Tuesday afternoon the lab called.

"The water's perfectly potable," said a beautiful, beautiful rippling voice. "We're giving you an A-1 rating."

"Yippee!" I yelled, turning on the kitchen taps and sticking my head under the faucet to drink that nectar from heaven. Then I went directly to the phone and invited Colonel Wilde to dinner.

As the season continued so did the problems. One night we ran out of the propane gas we used as cooking fuel, and for two hours I had to turn away all customers who wanted a hot dinner. Then Rebecca, our chef, took ill, and remembering that Alice Brock, who had formerly owned Alice's Restaurant, was Mary Pelke's daughter, and that she was at liberty, I called her. Alice is a tall, sensual woman with a strong personality. In our first confrontation I said (diplomatically, I thought), "Now, Alice, this is a French restaurant and in your place you cooked Russian and Middle Eastern food. Do you think you can manage it?"

"I can cook anything," she replied.

"Yes, but can you cook it French?" I pressed.

"Let me see your menu," she asked.

We studied it together.

"No problem," she scoffed. "But, Steve, I have to have carte

41

blanche in the choice of dishes, do my own ordering and work with my own assistant. Okay?"

"It will have the French touch though, Alice?" I asked nervously.

"Now, if you don't have faith in me . . ." She flailed her arms, looking like Phaedra hailing an Athenian ship.

Alice was a celebrity due to the Arlo Guthrie film *Alice's Restaurant*, and I felt her notoriety would be good publicity for Orpheus. "I have faith," I declared. And then, as she hadn't seemed to hear me, I repeated, "I said I have faith in you, Alice."

"And I need my own waiter, too," she added.

I had large posters printed proclaiming, "Alice Is Cooking At Orpheus Ascending!" Since Alice is an illustrator as well as a cook, I suggested she design the posters herself so that we could sell them in the gallery. (I suspect we took in more cash from the sale of the posters than we did from the sale of the food.)

Two days before she was to begin her "engagement" the cartons started arriving. Cases of buckwheat, groats and orzo. We had our second confrontation.

"Alice," I screamed, "you said you would keep to a French menu!"

"And you said you had faith!" she screamed back.

"I never heard of a French dish with buckwheat, groats or orzo," I countered.

She handed me a copy of a menu she had had printed. It was in French, though I had not heard of one dish.

"Faith," she repeated, and opening one of the refrigerators, she took out a chilled bottle of red wine. I gasped. The refrigerator was loaded with red wine. "Now, am I the chef or you?" she demanded, hugging the gallon bottle to her ample breast.

It was going to be impossible for me to take over the kitchen and still carry on with everything I had to do. Also, it had already been advertised that Alice was cooking for Orpheus.

"Okay, Alice," I agreed, "you're the chef, but I'm the boss. No chilled red wine. I abhor chilled red wine."

"I believe in the importance of wine in cooking—some in the stew, some in the cook." She laughed as she poured herself a glass.

The first night of her reign, plates filled with rice and pasta and beans sallied forth from the kitchen. I stormed through the swinging door and faced her. "You are serving rice *and* pasta *and* beans!" I shouted.

"What's wrong with that?" she demanded.

"To begin with, it's not French—and to end with, it's too heavy," I replied angrily.

"They don't have to eat all three," she said quite calmly, stirring a steaming pot, "but let them be there."

The next morning the kitchen was filled with containers of leftovers, which she was giving to all the employees to take home. When I complained, she said, "Leftovers toughen," which she stated as if it were an axiom. If that was the truth, it was a sorry one for me, since I was paying the bills. It is impossible to resent Alice though, for she is like the "mother-of-us-all." She is compulsive and wants to feed everyone in sight, believing no one should leave a table unless stuffed. I could see that our relationship had to be of short duration or I would go broke. Besides I didn't want to turn Orpheus into a Middle Eastern restaurant no matter how appropriate the name. So as soon as Rebecca mended, Alice and I came to a parting of the ways. (If the reader wants a poster of Alice cooking or a box of orzo, let them just write to me, I have a whole supply.)

With Rebecca's return, things ran more smoothly. Larri charmed all the guests and also Laura, who now walked around in what appeared to be a lovesick daze. But damned if she hadn't conquered her shyness! Doug forgave me for cutting the branch of the old oak tree, and the water flowed clear, plentiful and delicious. "Next year the swimming pool," I thought, now knowing how many prospective guests I was losing by not having one.

One sunny July morning a guest asked if she might have her coffee and croissants served on the screened verandah. It gave me an idea. If I could serve dinner on the verandah, our seating capacity would be doubled. Doug worked throughout the night scraping the floor and then painting it a bright blue. I ordered new screening and hung massive baskets of fuchsia from the beams. Then, taking a day off, I drove into New York, rented a U-Haul and returned with the small trailer full of tables and chairs that I had bought inexpensively on the Bowery.

The voluminous old maples hid the highway from "La Verandah," and the new screening kept out the insects. Soon tables on our renovated porch were considered the most desirable. The floor pitched terribly, though, and the glossy enamel made it slippery. The danger of a waiter or guest falling was now a constant worry as was the fear that the supports under the structure would collapse. I recalled the time when I was playing in a club on Fire Island and had been invited to a large cocktail party. As I approached the house, I saw the porch collapsing into the sand—chairs, glasses, people falling on top of each other. It could have been a great disaster, but thankfully, all the guests were so "loose" they were unharmed. The building inspector had pronounced my porch safe for forty-five people. Even so, I always seated any obese would-be diners inside. They never knew why. "Next year," I vowed, "I'll jack up the verandah. Just let us all get safely through this season."

But the fates seemed to be conspiring to make dining on the verandah less than tranquil. One windy night the stench from the overloaded septic tank drove all the outside diners in, but I had instructed the staff to tell guests at such times that a skunk had lodged under the porch and that that was the country!

Though our income was not yet enough to cover all our unbudgeted expenses, business boomed. After their concerts

Tanglewood musicians would come in and play. The great conductors like Bernstein and Ozawa had their favorite tables and their favorite dishes; actors from the Berkshire Playhouse down the road made Orpheus their hangout; Mabel Mercer, whom I consider the greatest American chanteuse, drove up from her home in nearby Chatham. I was heady with a sense of achievement and aware that Orpheus was growing into a gathering place for well-known as well as neophyte artists. The latter would get up to the piano and showcase their songs. I encouraged this and loved seeing the talent grow and become professional with exposure. I had not re-created Le Club de Paris but had created something special, personal and all-consuming for me.

Orpheus was more than a supper club, it was an inn, and since the rooms were small and the public areas few, the guests were soon on a first-name basis with each other and with me. I would close the bar and talk until the wee hours with some of them. An instant intimacy prevailed. My life suddenly seemed full, vital. Whatever frustrations had driven me to open a country inn were calmed. I had become dependent upon the relationships, the camaraderie of my club and the inn guests.

I recall that during that period, on an application for something or other, I filled in the blank that called for occupation with "innkeeper," where I would formerly have written "musician."

I was not at all sure that I liked this change in my lifestyle. I dreaded the end of summer which would signal the departure of my guests, and I decided to remain open on weekends throughout the winter, although with commuting to New York to teach three days a week at Carnegie Hall, it was not going to be easy.

As to the marriage I had hoped to save, it had grown successively worse in Stockbridge. I now knew it was just a matter of time before my wife and I would separate. When the last summer guest had left and we were alone, we agreed that divorce was the only course we could take. Even much earlier in the summer it had become quite clear to me that running an inn together was no panacea for a failing marriage. The added problems and close proximity exposed the incompatibility which had been only barely tolerable in less confining circumstances.

Once the decision was made I thought of what divorce would mean to me. The marriage had been over for a long time in any real sense, but I realized that inevitably the divorce would mean wrenching me from my son, limiting the time that we would have together. But there seemed to be no alternative.

We settled the details as quickly as possible and before the New England foliage season began I was alone. I don't think being alone is easy for anyone, but perhaps it is a little less difficult for an artist. Practicing the piano and learning new songs is an all-encompassing solitary job. So I plunged into my work; I began composing again, songs in French and a couple in English. As I played I was able to conjure up an imaginary audience, sense where laughter would follow an amusing line, visualize the tears that would fall during a sad song. I would flick on the spotlights and turn the sound system up high and try to picture the lounge crowded to capacity—just as I had done that day when Mary had first shown me the room.

That day seemed so long ago and the room was so different now. Beautiful, but deserted. The thirty comfortable armchairs seemed to need people to fill them. A couple of weeks before, when I had been so busy that customers had to be turned away, I cursed the smallness of the room; now it seemed enormous. My imaginary public kept fading out on me, deserting me. "Maybe it's the booze and I'm drunk," I told myself. Finally, in my sober days I could face the fact that I was just whistling in the dark. The truth was—I was lonely.

The foliage was beautiful that year. Doug's pruning had made our grounds glorious. Tourists drove up to photograph the flaming red maples that lined the road. Unable to bear the emptiness, I turned on the spotlights and hung an OPEN sign on Thursday nights.

With the departure of the tourists, a couple from town who owned a chain of local hardware stores called on me. They were atypical of Berkshire merchants, however. They were sophisticated and knowledgeable gourmets who had traveled extensively, their journeys always arranged like a connect-the-dots path between the best restaurants. Having recently instituted a gourmet cookware department in each branch, they decided on a weekly television program emanating from various local restaurants as a means of promoting sales of whisks and pressure cookers. I was invited to do one of their first shows.

They couldn't have chosen a better time, for the new project helped to assuage my loneliness. On the program, I had to assemble a crêpe batter, cook the crêpe, make a Mornay, add sautéed shrimp, stuff the crêpe, bake and present it, all in fifteen minutes—twelve, when you eliminated the time for commercials. I practiced just as I would practice the piano.

I find cooking eases tension, in any case. It demands the utmost attention. There is no time for self-pity, especially if one is preparing a complicated dish. I worked to make the act as professional as a network show and looked forward to the opportunity to be on camera. I even enjoyed the technicians, announcers and, particularly, the enthusiasm of the fledgling director who invaded my kitchen. I relished the off-camera floodlights and the cables underfoot. I was surrounded by theater people and I was, however minor, a star.

The first program was well received and soon I was asked to do a repeat. For my second show I decided to write my own script, intending to outdo the first performance as well as to accent the elegance of Orpheus. I chose to prepare a salmon mousse, a dish popular at our summer brunches, which was made entirely in a blender—a new line for the hardware store. I needed a gimmick for the show and decided to do my

47

cooking in a tuxedo. I would enter and tell "Mrs. Main Street" that she need not look like a scullery maid at her next dinner party. She could hostess the cocktail hour in a gown and then, excusing herself, retire to the kitchen where she would work without an apron. She would reappear a short time later, mousse in hand, as splendidly dressed as ever.

Prior to the taping session I chopped all the ingredients, arranged them in bowls, and rehearsed my glib dialogue. I then opened the program seated at the Steinway, singing "You're the Cream in My Coffee" in French, thinking privately of myself as the Noël Coward of the kitchen. During the first commercial I moved to the kitchen to begin the actual cooking. Everything had been set up, so I nonchalantly added the finely chopped onions and the sour cream into the blender. I chopped the fresh dill and squeezed a quartered lemon with unbelievable insouciance. Next I added a poached fileted salmon from a silver tray and the last of the exotic spices to the blender. As I had rehearsed with the director, I was then to turn on the machine, and while it churned noisily, there would be a taped commercial.

But things were not to go as planned. I turned on the blender—but I forgot to put on the top. Salmon mousse splattered everything, including my tuxedo. The young director wanted to reshoot, but I had a better idea. After the commercial he had planned to say, "And now we return to Orpheus Ascending and Maestro Steve Citron," but I convinced him instead to move the camera directly back to me. So I donned what appeared to be a fresh jacket (actually the old one wiped clean) and said, "Keeping a spare jacket or evening dress in the kitchen is as important to the success of your dinner as cooking in sufficient quantity." I smiled as I buttoned the tuxedo and proceeded suavely with the recipe.

The program produced the biggest response in the station's history. It had something to do with the appeal that Julia Child has—her humanness. Amateur cooks always like to see professionals make mistakes. Every time Julia drops a chicken on the floor or turns out a flat soufflé, the television audience gains new courage to attempt the recipe themselves.

With her inn closed for the season, Stephanie Barber found time to come over on the weekends and sing her deep-throated ballads in French and German. I now had a friend in Stef, a kindred spirit. One dreary Friday night in November when the snow was falling thicker than the frogs had been in the swimming pool, it looked as though we might not have one customer. That had never happened before. I called Stef. "I can't stand it!" I told her. "Come over, bring some people. I'll make it a private party."

Before she arrived, a few people did finally wend their way up the driveway, terrified to continue onward in the storm and happy to see our lights. Stef's friend, writer Joan Mills, staggered in frozen and breathless. "Steffi's bringing Anne Edwards and Jim Pitt's coming," she said, as I escorted her into the lounge and to the fireplace.

"Who's Anne Edwards?" I asked.

"A novelist."

"Literary type, huh?"

"Well, she doesn't wear tweeds or smoke a pipe," Joan wisecracked.

Soon Stef pulled her little Renault into our slippery parking lot and threaded her way carefully to the door accompanied by a lady swathed in black.

"*Mon amie* Anne, *mon ami* Steve," Stef introduced.

The stranger removed her coat but was still swathed in black. She was wearing a jersey dress that was hooded, long-sleeved and high-necked. She had a trace of an English accent. I seated Stef's party at a round table by the fireplace. Anne pushed back the hood of her dress and mounds of auburn hair cascaded down. In the light of the fire a few melted drops of snow that clung to her face were reflected like sequins. I glanced at her, hoping she would not catch me looking. Pure Hollywood. High cheekbones, black eyes, generous mouth. She was beautiful but she didn't know it. For one moment our eyes met and from then on, throughout the evening, she kept her head down, talking to the others at her table.

I drew out my first set, delaying that moment when I finally sat down at her table. "Miss Hollywood" was studying the reflections in her glass of hot coffee and brandy. Piqued, I moved to another table. Stef sang and then Jim accompanied himself on the guitar in songs of the twenties. I followed with my second set, digging deeply into my past with a Noël Coward song that I had not sung for a long time.

Life is often rough and tumble
For a humble *diseur* . . .

All the pent-up emotion of the past few months was pouring out of me. I continued . . .

I think if only
Somebody splendid really needed me . . .

They were rising at Stef's table. "Miss Hollywood" had the hood back up and her auburn hair tucked in. Her brow was furrowed. It was obvious she didn't like the place or me. I finished the song and saw them to the door, kissing Stef on the cheek and extending my hand to the lady in black.

"Promise me you'll come back?" I said, as she drew quickly away. Sparks had ignited at that touch and I wondered if she felt them, too. She did not promise to return.

The following Sunday night Stef called.

"Are you leaving at that same ridiculous hour?" she asked.

I had been driving into New York every Monday morning, leaving at six-thirty in order to give a ten o'clock lesson. "Yes, you riding in with me?" I asked, anxious for company.

"If I may. And, Stephen, you remember Anne Edwards?"

I acknowledged that I did.

"She has to go into New York, too. Can she ride with us?"

"I don't mind," I said, trying to cover how apprehensive I was. "Where does she live?"

"In Stockbridge. On Christian Hill."

"In that case, I'll pick you up at six-fifteen and we'll go over there together."

"Wouldn't it be shorter to pick her up first and just scoot out from my place to the highway?"

"No," I lied, adding quickly, "bring your music. We'll discuss it on the ride."

"My music!" Stef lamented. "I can't even see the highway at that hour."

The alarm went off at five-thirty, but I awoke before it. Usually, I dressed in sport clothes, but that morning, not only did I trim my mustache and my hair, I even wore a tie.

Stef and I pulled into the driveway on Christian Hill. "La Edwards" wiped the steam from the frosted glass of her front window and indicated she would be right out. When she appeared she carried a brightly flowered suitcase and wore huge sunglasses and a white wool coat, but no scarf on her mass of hair. She flashed a smile as she got into the back of the car, and I thought, "Great teeth, probably capped." I ran my tongue over my own teeth and decided I needed a visit to the dentist.

Stef and I talked music most of the trip while "La Edwards" busied herself shuffling through a sheaf of papers. I could see her in the rear-view mirror, curled like a cat in the corner of the back seat. Once, when our eyes met in the mirror, both of us quickly looked away. I dropped the two of them off at Carnegie Hall, and before they left, I said to Stef, "I return Thursday, early. Want to ride back?"

"I have to go back tonight, *mon cher*, but maybe *mon amie*..."

I gave "La Edwards" my phone number.

On Thursday morning there was a message from "La Ed-

wards" on the answering machine. "This is Anne Edwards,"
she began brightly. "If your offer still stands, I'd like to ride
back with you. I'm at the Gotham Hotel. Please call and tell
me what time."

Trapped. Alone for three hours with a career lady—and one
who sent my temperature up at that. "You're scared, Citron,"
I admitted. Then I girded my loins and called "La Edwards."
I told her I would pick her up in fifteen minutes and that she
should be ready and waiting downstairs.

As we drove from the city to Stockbridge that winter morning—car windows were shut tight, exterior sound cut out, the
roads virtually deserted—I felt as if we were secluded from the
world. Anne was easy to talk to in such a private, intimate
atmosphere. I found myself telling her about my marriage,
talking about my past, going far back. There was a compulsive
need to fill her in, to force her to know as much about me as
the drive would allow. She made no judgments but sat there
wrapped in a car blanket, leaning back against the upholstered
seat, eyes wide with attention. I called her Anne, then Annie.
I thought she'd probably object to the familiarity but she
didn't. I felt an overwhelming intimacy—as though the car
were a bedroom.

"How did you get to Stockbridge?" I asked, about halfway
there, wanting to hear her voice, wanting to know as much
about her as I had revealed about myself.

"Well," she began, after a long moment of consideration,
"one morning, in the South of France . . ." She straightened
and turned to me. "I lived in Europe for sixteen years," she
explained. "My second husband was a British subject and a film
producer and there was a large film colony on the Côte d' Azur.
Things had been going badly between us and one morning I
awoke abruptly and knew that my marriage was over and that
I wanted more than anything else to go home, to touch some
of my roots. The problem was that so few of my family and

friends remained that home merely seemed to imply the States
. . . *anywhere* in the States."

She laughed softly and readjusted her position, legs now
tucked under her, arms wrapped around herself, body turned
to me. "It was really madness," she exclaimed. "Cathy, my
teenage daughter, was home from school for the Christmas
holidays and I shouted at her down the long hallway that
separated our bedrooms—'We're going home, baby!' Cathy
poked her head out of her doorway and rather sleepily asked,
'Where?' as though the word had never entered her vocabulary
before. 'Get an atlas,' I called back, 'I'll show you.' We sat in
the huge old French kitchen with the atlas between us. 'Any
place in particular strike your fancy?' I asked. 'New England,'
she replied. 'I've been thinking of going to college there if we
can afford it.'

"She explained that she had four or five schools in mind, all
of them in Connecticut, New Hampshire, Massachusetts or
Vermont. I turned to an enlarged map of New England,
confiding to her that I wanted to find someplace where she
could come home on weekends and where her brother Michael
could visit frequently from Washington, D.C., where he
lived."

Anne's eyes misted and she sank down in the seat. "She's a
terribly sensitive kid. Exceptionally pretty." She laughed nervously. "She also reminded me that I wasn't exactly a recluse
and that I would do best to find a place with some kind of a
creative and intellectual society. Anyway, we both pressed in
cioser to study the map, and several mugs of coffee later we had
selected four towns—Petersborough, New Hampshire, where
MacDowell, a writing community, was located; Woodstock,
New York; Hanover, New Hampshire, where I had friends; and
Stockbridge, Massachusetts, because it was near Tanglewood
and I had once been to a concert there when I was a child.
Cathy suggested we return to the States and visit each one but

—oh Lord, I was in a hurry to get moving! I decided to write the chamber of commerce of each town. The first one that answered would be *home.*"

"Pretty illogical, but why not?" I laughed.

"Exactly! So we decided to take a boat—because I would never have been able to afford the overweight on a plane. That afternoon I wrote letters to the four chambers of commerce asking for information on local hotels or inns, real estate companies and kennels. I have two rather nutty poodles," she explained. "The next morning I called American Express in Nice and had them book passage for the three of us—oh, yes, *us* included Alex, the twenty-two-year-old Filipino who lived with us as cook-cum-handyman-cum-friend."

"Stef told me he was a fabulous Chinese cook—and that you were, too," I mentioned.

"I'm really Swedish-Hungarian, which I think makes me a bit of a Martian and a terribly eclectic cook."

"Go on with your story," I nudged, sorry I had interrupted and somewhat in awe of how she could weave a tale, filling in all the details. It was as though she were reading from an invisible book, but her words came honestly and openly. "I've found my Scheherazade," I thought.

"We began to pack and pack and pack. Between us we had forty-seven assorted boxes, suitcases and trunks. Mind you, we had no idea where we were headed, but eight days after I had posted the letters I received three replies—all from Stockbridge. The first was from the Red Lion Inn offering to accommodate us on a weekly basis; the second was from Steffi giving a list of available houses; and the third was from a vet with pictures of his kennels. We wrote 'Stockbridge, Massachusetts' on all forty-seven baggage tags."

"And that was it?" I asked, amazed.

"That was it."

*   *   *

The next week Stef and Anne drove down with me again but only Anne made the return trip. I asked her about her ex-husband.

"He was a very ordered man," she replied, and sat there quietly for a long time, her hands folded in her lap, the seat belt attached to the door handle because she couldn't stand confinement. "I'm pretty careless," she finally added. "I mean, I forget where I put things and leave things where they shouldn't be." She glanced up at me, eyes wide with confession, "I leave the cap off the toothpaste," she admitted.

"He didn't approve?"

"Hated it."

"I leave the cap off the toothpaste, too," I told her. "Seems like such a useless effort to replace it."

"Well, my husband hated it," she repeated.

"Isn't it really," I told her, "that when you're in love you find leaving the cap off the toothpaste an endearing trait in your partner. You assume the other is preoccupied or worried and you have sympathy. But when you're not in love, it just seems a sloppy habit."

"I don't think even if my husband had really loved me he would have loved me leaving the cap off the toothpaste." She smiled.

"You could leave the cap off my toothpaste anytime," I said.

"I've never had quite that same kind of proposition before." She laughed.

The following week Stef didn't drive down. A deeper feeling now existed between Anne and me. We found we agreed on music, politics, children and family. Most of all, we shared a kinship in our abhorrence of hostility. Neither of us seemed to be able to face that, and both of us felt we had been married to partners who thrived on it.

At the end of the trip, Anne gave me, a bit shyly, a copy of an early book of hers. As I dropped her off at Christian Hill

55

that Thursday, she said, "This is a very important book to me."
The book talked about courage of convictions, and as I read it
I knew it was autobiographical.

I called her before the weekend was over. We talked about
the book, plans to drive down to New York together on Monday morning and some problems that my son, Lex, seemed to
be having at school. "I love you, you know," I said before I
disconnected, surprised to hear myself utter the words.

"Thank you," she replied, and hung up before I could say
anything else. We were acting like a couple of teenagers. It was
madness.

One of my students and good friends called me in New York
that week and suggested that we go to hear Mabel Mercer sing
at the St. Regis after our lesson. I decided to ask Anne to join
us, hoping she'd love Mabel as I did. She did. After the performance we left my friend and walked back to Anne's hotel.

"I'll see you to the elevator," I said. Then as the elevator
doors opened, I said, "I'll see you to your door." And at her
door I asked, "Can I stay the night?"

There it was—*the moment*, you could say. She opened the
door. A double bed dominated the small room. "This isn't a
casual date," I thought. "You walk through that door and,
Steve, you are *involved*."

"Annie," I asked, cupping her chin in my hand and looking
her square in those deep brown eyes, "Are you ready for this?"

Her answer was slow and sure. "Yes," she said. "Are you?"

I studied the sincerity in her eyes, the tenderness of her
smile. "No, I'm not. Right now I think it was a mistake ending
up here. Hell, I'm still fighting the lawyers over the divorce and
getting daily bitch calls from my estranged wife. Divorce is
shit," I said harshly, and drew back. We stood silently in the
corridor, neither of us sure of what the other expected. "Good
night," she said. I kissed her lightly on the cheek, mumbled
some inane apology and tore down the hall for a fast exit.

I walked back through the cold, late-night streets to stay at my Carnegie studio. At that hour, Seventh Avenue is Whore's Row. A girl smiled prettily. "Got a match?" she asked. I kept on walking. She drew alongside me. "Maybe you didn't hear me," she said. "I asked if you got a match." She had a young, peasant face and was well built. Stacked. I turned to light her cigarette. A heavy arm came from behind and caught me around the neck.

"Whatcha got? Let's have it," a deep voice growled in my ear. I reached in my pocket for my wallet. "Your watch, too," the man ordered. He jerked my hand painfully behind me. I resisted momentarily—an instinct. We were in front of a closed parking lot. There wasn't a soul near enough to help. Shouting would have done me no good. He ripped the watch off my wrist and pushed me back and to the ground before both of them disappeared down the street.

Slowly, I got to my feet. My jacket was torn and my wrist badly wrenched, but neither my fingers nor any other bones seemed to be broken. Still, it was going to be hell to play the piano for a while. There wasn't a policeman in sight, so I dusted myself off and continued on toward the studio, all the while berating myself because I hadn't stayed with Anne. "You're an idiot, Citron," I thought. "You would have gone with that whore if her accomplice hadn't mugged you."

Exhausted, I made it to the studio, took a shower and tried to sleep. Impossible. My hand was killing me and my thoughts were troubled. Daylight was slow in coming. I paced back and forth in front of my pianos. Finally, I called the operator to see what time it was. Six-forty. I called Anne, waking her, and told her I had to return earlier than I thought and that she would have to take the bus back.

"I'll get dressed right away and go with you," she said.

"No, it's a crazy hour," I alibied, not wanting her to see me in the state I was in.

"Something's the matter," she said. "I can hear it in your voice."

57

"I had a small accident," I lied.

"Pick me up in fifteen minutes," she said and then disconnected.

The garage wasn't open yet and I walked over to the hotel. She was standing there in the freezing wind, her flowered suitcase at her feet, her hands tucked deep into the pockets of the white wool coat, her red hair flying, looking as she did on our first ride from Stockbridge. She ran over to me, leaving the suitcase on the sidewalk when she saw me coming, taking my hand as she reached me. I winced.

"Don't ask any questions," I said. "Let's find someplace to have coffee while we wait for the garage to open."

Fifty-fifth Street was lined with early-morning delivery trucks. "I don't know if I'm more an idiot or a bastard," I said, after telling her what had happened. "I run from love like a crazy man right smack into disaster!"

We were standing in front of a luncheonette and the wind was whipping around us. Anne's eyes were filled with compassion and tears. She turned her back to the wind, facing me. I drew her into my arms and we kissed. There we stood, locked in an embrace, pedestrians stepping around us, truckdrivers gaping and the people inside the luncheonette watching us through the window. Finally, we moved apart.

"I don't think you're either," she said.

"Either what?"

"An idiot or a bastard."

"Let's go in and have that coffee," I replied. "I have this sensational feeling that we're in love and I think we should celebrate."

Anne spent that night with me at Orpheus. "If only I could accept a simple pragmatic viewpoint," I thought, as I left her in my bed and went down to the kitchen to make us some coffee. It was Friday morning and the inn would be closed until afternoon. The problem was, I had never felt such fulfillment. I cursed the simplicity of it all. I loved her and wanted her always to share my bed. "What could be more natural and ordinary?" I asked myself.

I came back into the bedroom with two mugs and a steaming carafe of coffee. Her high-heeled shoes had been kicked off halfway from the door to the bed. The musky scent of her cologne filled the room, and on the floor by the bed was her velvet dress, its bright blue catching the early-morning winter sun as it came through the open blinds. She was still asleep and I stood over her, feeling that her auburn hair had always belonged on my pillow. I knew that I was going to ask her to come live with me. I roused her gently and she turned to me like a sleepy child.

"Let's have sex," I murmured into her neck.

"Let's make love," she whispered back.

We made love.

She left around noon because her daughter was coming home for the weekend. We made plans to go into New York together that following Monday morning. It seemed a long time to wait, but perhaps it would give me time to think it all out. It was Friday and guests were due by early evening. There was shopping and cooking to do, and Lex would be arriving after school. By midafternoon I was in the kitchen, two pâtés and a stockpot of onion soup made, and was preparing the Mornay for the crêpes when the doorbell rang and a young willowy girl with long dark hair swept into the kitchen. The large black dog with her pushed her aside and immediately stood on its hind legs to sniff the pâté on the work counter.

"No dogs," I bellowed, and whipped the pâté up past the dog's head. It barked and danced precariously close to my upstretched hands.

The girl put down a cookie tray wrapped in foil and grabbed the dog's collar. "Nikki!" she reprimanded. "She's only a puppy." She went on to explain, "Someone deserted her and I'm keeping her at school. She just hasn't had time to be trained yet."

"Dogs are against the health code," I growled.

She dragged the dog across the room and out to the rear kitchen. I heard the door slam. Then she returned. I had just put the pâté back and was looking under the foil at what was on the cookie tin.

"Egg rolls and fried wontons," she said.

"You must be Cathy," I exclaimed, and then stood back to take a good look at her. She was quite beautiful, with dark brown silken hair, a cameo profile, sturdy-looking yet reed-slim. A smile flickered and she laughed as easily as her mother did.

"There are some sauces out in the car," she continued. "I couldn't carry everything in at once." She started out the swinging door.

"Cathy . . ." I called. She turned. "I lost my temper," I apologized.

"I noticed," she replied, and then was gone.

I stood there in the kitchen thinking to myself, "Now, why would Anne send Chinese food to a French restaurant?" I mumbled, "If I wanted any wontons on the menu, or any egg rolls either, I would bloody well make them myself!"

Cathy returned with the sauces, the Labrador again at her heels. "I can't help it," she protested. "She's hard to hold back when your hands are filled." At that moment the black dog began to wag its long curved tail furiously and a stack of salad plates was swept off a shelf.

"I'm sorry," Cathy said, *really sorry,* but as I said, she's only a puppy. I'll clean those broken dishes up for you."

"It's all right. The housekeeper can do it later."

"Sure?"

"Sure."

She smiled disarmingly, and then began to wrinkle her retroussé nose. "Something's burning," she murmured.

"What did you say?"

"Something on the stove is burning." She ran over and pushed the pot off the flame. "Oh, it *was* a Mornay sauce. You shouldn't cook a Mornay unless you're going to watch it every single minute."

I went over to the stove. The sauce was ruined. "Damn it! I'll have to start all over again," I cursed. There was a crash in the back kitchen. "And please," I asked as politely as I could, "*please* take that dog out of here."

Before she left she poked her head back through the door. "Not to worry," she crooned. "It was only the metal meat grinder. I put it in the sink."

I started a fresh pot of Mornay, and had just reached the moment of truth when you have to get the cream to boiling point and mix it into the roux, when the front doorbell rang. Someone had entered the bar. "Who is it?" I called.

A burly deliveryman came into the kitchen. "Where do you want them?" he asked.

"Want what?"

"The plants. Looks like you could start a jungle."

"There must be a mistake. I didn't order any plants."

He glanced down at the clipboard he was holding. "This here Orrifice Ascending?"

"Orpheus Ascending," I corrected angrily.

"They're yours then."

"I didn't order any plants. I don't want them. And I'm not going to pay for them!" I shouted.

"You don't have to. Says here charge to Edwards, Christian Hill. Hey, Mister, something's burning."

The Mornay had boiled over onto the stove for a second time.

"Where shall I put them?" he asked again.

"I don't care. In the bar, I guess," I said weakly and began

61

to clean the stove. About five minutes later he came back into the kitchen and asked me to sign his clipboard. I decided to look at the delivery before I signed.

Plants were everywhere—on the stools, the bar, the floor, the tables and the windowsills; big plants, small plants, trees, vines, flowering bushes.

"You going to sign or not?" the deliveryman asked as I stood aghast in the doorway.

I signed and he left, weaving his way through the rows of plants like an experienced jungle guide!

I made my own way to the bar, took down a bottle of Scotch and poured myself a tall one. There was a note tied to a big aspidistra that faced me across the bar.

"I wanted to give you life," it said, in a graceful, slanted script, "as you gave life to me. I love you. Anne."

I leaned across and said to that big aspidistra, "Who needs you? Haven't I enough responsibility without worrying about watering schedules and fertilizers?"

I downed the Scotch and poured another.

Anything that's beautiful takes caring for, I decided. I picked up the aspidistra and struggled to carry it into the sitting room, where I placed it in the sunny bay window.

"I gave her life," I kept thinking over and over again as I distributed the plants all over the inn. No one had ever said anything so beautiful to me before.

"Must have cost a pretty penny for all them plants!" Mrs. Gretchner, the new housekeeper, said when she arrived to get the rooms in order for the weekend guests.

The Weisses were the first to arrive. They had been to the inn many times before and we had, by now, become good friends. As I showed them to their room, Johanna Weiss commented, "The place looks alive now. Maybe it's all those beautiful plants." She smiled at me. "Or maybe it's you."

"I'm in love," I told her.

"That's not so bad," her husband, Danny, said. "You could be married."

We had four rooms booked that weekend. Besides Johanna and Danny Weiss, there was a proper Bostonian couple, a pair of young honeymooners and a couple who had called saying they were "roommates" and wanted a "congenial" place to stay.

Mrs. Gretchner had comments about everyone who passed through Orpheus. When she came to me that Saturday morning, she knitted her eyebrows and whispered, "They slept in the same single bed. Two peas in a pod. Two grown men in one small bed! Saves changing a couple of sheets. I guess there's some good in all things evil."

I continued stacking my music next to the piano.

"Honeymooners aren't up yet," she chattered on. "They're going to miss breakfast. Can't live on love, someone should tell them. Well, guess you're only young once." She poked me in the ribs as I went to pass by her. I was spared listening to any more of Mrs. Gretchner's "epigrams" by the appearance of the Bostonian gentleman, jam spattered down the front of his tweed pants.

"Might I have a napkin?" he inquired. "I've been a bit clumsy."

"We don't serve napkins at breakfast," Mrs. Gretchner stated flatly.

"Of course we do, Mrs. Gretchner," I said, running to get one for him.

When Mrs. Gretchner and I were alone again, I asked her, "What's this about no napkins at breakfast?"

"A penny saved is a penny earned," she admonished. "Waste not, want not."

"Where else have you been saving me pennies?" I pressed.

"I stretch the orange juice by adding a little water," she said proudly. "And if you don't put an extra roll of toilet paper in

63

the bathrooms they'll use less." She placed the flat of her hand on my shoulder. "Mr. Citron, you're young in this business. I've worked in hotels and motels all my life."

"Well, this isn't a hotel or motel." I bristled. "This is a small, elegant inn where our guests pay good prices for a feeling of largesse and luxe and I intend to see that they receive it."

Mrs. Gretchner shrugged and waddled off.

The next day as I drove up the driveway on my return from marketing I noticed something different about the inn, though I didn't know what. It was clear, however, the moment I got inside. There were no curtains. Anywhere.

Mrs. Gretchner greeted me with a wide smile.

"What's happened to the curtains?" I asked.

"Didn't look perky enough so I took them down and washed them. Some people don't think about keeping a house clean and some people do," she replied. "I always say cleanliness is next to godliness."

Numbly I followed her into the kitchen. It was filled with curtains. Twenty rooms of curtains drying everywhere on every conceivable makeshift clothesline.

"Are you sure you can get these back up in time for the guests tomorrow?" I asked.

"Of course. They're wash and wear. No need to iron them."

"I don't mean that. I mean how are you going to know which windows they fit? Every window in the inn is a different size and so is each pair of curtains."

"Don't worry, Mr. Citron. I'll figure it out."

Mrs. Gretchner spent the next day frantically trying to re-hang the curtains, but nothing seemed to match. She countered my anger by grumbling that the fabric was not shrink-proof, and that was why nothing fit.

"Don't ever do anything like that without discussing it with me first," I said.

"But don't they look clean?" she replied.

Anne had been slowly moving in during the week and, by

the following Friday, the transfer was more or less complete. Portable bookshelves now lined the walls of my bedroom, bright books neatly stacked on them. Another chest of drawers and a desk were brought in, and the bureau top became a maze of perfume bottles, family pictures and other memorabilia. A full-length mirror had been hung behind the door, and my clothes were jammed tightly to one side of the closet to make room for an incredible number of long red and black gowns. The bathroom was hung with a profusion of huge, bright plants; red towels were draped over the racks; a makeshift dressing table was pushed into a corner and crowded with baskets of lipsticks, hairpins and chopsticks (which I did not understand). Both bathroom and bedroom seemed to have shrunk, but I had never felt so happy in them before.

Lex was due home from school that afternoon, since he spent the weekends with me, the rest of the time with his mother. We had decided that for this weekend Anne would sleep in the room adjoining ours. As I placed her robe and slippers there for her, I thought about the dishonesty of the move and knew I would have to tell Lex the truth soon. But how do you explain to a five-year-old that his daddy is in love and will henceforth be sleeping in the same bed with a lady he has never met?

It wasn't long before the door slammed as Lex came in, dropping lunch pail, jacket and colored papers as he ran through the house in a rush to tell me about the new hamster they had in school. I had bought him a model ship and excitedly he set to helping me build it. I mentioned that we were going out to dinner that evening with a lady friend of mine and that he would have a chance to practice his pulling-out-the-chair technique and all the other things I had taught him about politeness. He was more interested in the model ship.

We took Lex for an early dinner at the Red Lion Inn, where he could have all our attention without the distractions dining at Orpheus presented. As we passed through the lobby, which is the gossip center of Stockbridge, there were whispers and buzzings. Lex was oblivious to it all, playing word games with Anne and showing off in general. They had taken to each other and that was important to me.

"Kiss Annie goodnight," I suggested after we had returned and before I took him up to bed. He drew shyly away.

"That's okay," Anne said, smiling. "I'll take a raincheck."

As he climbed into bed he said to me, "I'm sure you're going to tell me the story of 'The Owl and the Pussycat.' "

"Why are you so sure I'll tell you that one?" I asked.

"It's the shortest one. You always tell it to me when you are in a hurry," he replied.

"Why do you think I'm in a hurry?"

"You told Annie you'd be right down."

I told him the longest story I could think of, and as I kissed him goodnight, I asked, "Do you like Annie?"

"She's okay," he answered. "She makes good paper hats."

I rejoined her in the lounge and for the first time I felt a need for my own quarters, a place where we could be private. Behind us was the sound of the hi-fi, dishes clattering and the conversation of perfect strangers. "I'm sorry about the kiss," I whispered.

"He sees me as competition to his mother and he's loyal. You wouldn't want him any other way," she said, taking my hand.

The following morning Lex came into my bed with his big storybook. "I'm in love with Annie," I told him, "and when two people are in love, they sleep in the same bed."

"Does that mean you don't love me?"

"No, of course not!"

"Well, how come you never sleep in my bed?"

I was spared more complicated explanations by the ringing of the telephone. Rebecca had fallen from her horse, broken her shoulder and would not be able to cook that night—and probably not for several weeks to come. "I know you have that

66

wedding scheduled for tomorrow and I'm awfully upset about it," she commiserated. "Maybe Alice will help—or someone from the Red Lion."

The wedding! Two local residents were being married on Sunday morning and were having a noon reception for thirty-five at Orpheus. It was to be my first venture into catering. In summertime I was staffed to serve that many entrées at once, but in the spring with no cook and a short staff, how would I manage the bar and also the quantity of crêpes the party had ordered?

I brought Anne a pot of coffee and some croissants. She looked beautiful, propped up in bed, a writing pad on her knee.

"I have to rush off," I said. "Rebecca is ill and I have to market and cook for tonight as well as prepare for a wedding reception to be held here in the morning."

"A wedding? How marvelous! I'll help." She threw back the covers and swung her legs over the edge of the bed.

I pushed her gently back. "You stay here and write. It's my problem and I can manage it."

Later in the afternoon I picked up the mail at the post office, which is the heart of Stockbridge. The postmaster handed me my letters and said, "Oh, I guess you'll be wanting this, too." He held out a packet of letters. "They're for Miss Edwards." There was no leer, no gossipy poke in the ribs. He was a postal officer seeing that the letters reach the addressee as expeditiously as possible. We had probably been the topic of conversation in the town for twenty-four hours and that was it. Stockbridge had now accepted the fact that we were living together.

When I returned, Mrs. Gretchner was still juggling curtains from window to window. "It's like a Chinese puzzle," she said. I withdrew quickly to the kitchen to avoid killing her and splattering her nice, clean white curtains with her own blood.

April is mud season and the tourists avoid Stockbridge for sunnier climes. We had a few regulars who were to be counted on but otherwise business was not good. I had handwritten a special short menu and instructed our new waiter, an elegant Iranian named Yousef, on how to prepare and serve the entrées. In that way we were able to get through Saturday and concentrate on the wedding party.

I directed each song I sang that night to Anne, shuffling through my black book, choosing titles that would make her respond. She listened with a kind of special intensity and later discussed each selection in detail with me. No one close to me had ever been so involved in my music before. After everyone had left, it seemed the most natural thing in the world for us to share the task of turning out all the lights together. And as I led the way up the stairs, I thought of us as a couple who had just said goodnight to the last guest at a party.

I began work at dawn on the wedding brunch—making crêpes and fresh Mornay, poaching fruit, shelling peas. At nine Anne stuck her head into the kitchen.

"Can I help?" she asked.

"Go back to your muse," I ordered.

The best man called. The wedding party would be arriving a half-hour early. Now, half an hour does not seem like much when you are ready, but if you aren't, it is a catastrophe. I tried reaching Yousef to tell him to come in early, but there was no answer.

I called Anne on the intercom. "I'm accepting your offer of help," I said. She was down in two minutes.

She stood in the doorway observing the bedlam and then asked, "Have you got a chopstick?"

"A chopstick? We're serving French food."

"Never mind," she replied as she grabbed an oyster fork and stuck it in the hair she had piled atop her head. Miraculously the fork held it in place. So that was why we had chopsticks in the bathroom!

She rolled up the sleeves of her blouse and began clearing the front kitchen of dirty dishes, putting them into the back kitchen. "Where's the salad bowl?" she asked. I pointed. "My goodness, it's huge," she commented as she tried to fit it into the refrigerator. "Keeps the salad crisper. These the greens?" I nodded. She piled her arms with them and managed to make it safely to the sink, and without saying a word she began her kitchen maid's task of washing the salad.

Yousef arrived with the guests, ushering them into the sitting room and the gallery, and then came back into the kitchen. "My God," he said. "The groom must be close to eighty and the bride and the rest of the guests aren't much younger!"

"We need time," I complained. "Offer them a glass of champagne on the house."

Yousef came back with the champagne untouched.

"They want orange juice," he announced.

"Mix the juice with the champagne," Anne suggested.

Soon there was laughter in the other room, and the sound of ragtime being played poorly on the piano.

"Let's have our own celebration," I said to Anne, pouring each of us a glass of champagne. She had been elbow-deep in the lettuce and she dried her hands. We drained our glasses and then she went back to washing the lettuce, looking quite insane with that oyster fork stuck in her hair and one of our red tablecloths tied around her like an apron. She sang along to the clanky sound of the piano—a child playing grownup in that oversized world of the restaurant kitchen.

PART

TWO

The first time I saw him, he was seated at an enormous piano singing, moving with incredible agility from the intense melancholy of a Piaf song to the flip sophistication of Cole Porter. I was immediately taken with his appearance—the rough-hewn face, the tumbled mass of coarse gray hair, the dark eyes that seemed not to miss a thing. And I was moved by his vibrant voice, the full-throated laugh, the way he phrased a lyric, his involvement in his music. I remember finding it difficult to exchange glances with him when he sat down to talk to us. Emotion clung to him like the musky scent he wore. He spoke about the bad shape of business and the lack of adventurousness of those Berkshire residents who did not stampede through his door. There was no self-pity; it was more anger and impatience that things were not proceeding as he had expected. His knee touched mine under the table and I quickly drew back and turned away.

"I'm not ready," I told myself. It had been only ten months since my own marriage had broken and I had returned from a long residence in Europe. In Stockbridge I had been occupied with my writing, my teenage daughter Cathy and the constant flow of visitors to the little red brick schoolhouse I had rented in the Berkshires.

By fall that year, however, Cathy had left for college, and except for friends and my two poodles I was alone. My son Michael, on a visit to Stockbridge, zeroed in on the truth.

We walked together quietly through the wooded paths behind the house, turning up a dirt road thickly matted with
fallen leaves. Bowed branches plumed in flaming red shaded
the path which led to a well.

"It's not enough, Mom, is it?" Michael asked, as he dodged
a low branch.

"Of course it is," I said defensively.

"Maybe you should give up the Berkshires and move into
the city," he persisted.

"Which one?"

"New York."

"No way."

"What happens when the snows come and Cathy can't get
home every weekend and your flow of guests turns into a
trickle?"

"I'll love it," I insisted.

Michael has remarkable blue-green eyes that seem to see
right through you. "Convince me," he said, turning those eyes
directly upon me.

"I don't have to. It's *my* life."

My son pumped water for me as I cupped my hands and
splashed my face with it.

"Just keep in mind," he said quietly, "that it's no big thing
if you find it's a mistake to stay here."

Until I walked into Orpheus and met Steve I felt reasonably
sure that I could be happy living alone, and had our lives never
crossed, that might have been the case. Now, living together,
sharing his life at the inn, I was aware how incomplete that life
would have been.

The kids took the news fantastically well, perhaps with even
a sigh of relief.

"What would you think if I moved in with Steve and helped
him run Orpheus?" I asked Cathy as soon as my mind was
made up.

"You've always run an inn, only you never got paid for it," she replied. Then she put her arm around my shoulders. "I couldn't subscribe to a double standard," she said. "If I meet someone, I'll want to live with him for a long time before I consider marriage." We clung together and when we broke apart she said, "I'm glad you're not going to be here alone. It was kind of a heavy thing for me."

So here I was—the innkeeper's lady, and loving it.

It was still winter when we first began to live together and the inn was open only on weekends. I had scheduled editorial meetings in New York for a new book, and Steve and I were able to go into the city each week, returning for two days alone before the inn was transformed into a public place. On those two nights we would dine in front of the sitting-room hearth or light the fire in our room and watch the flames from the bed. We would take walks through the snow and come back to our own bar where we would fix ourselves any drink imaginable. There was music in every room downstairs, and selecting a record was like being given free rein in a record shop. On the weekends I felt, in some ways, like someone who owned a huge country estate and gave lavish parties. For the two of us—a man and a woman who had each had two failed marriages and yet knew love was still possible—sharing, living as inseparably as we did that first winter and spring at the inn, was an idyll, a fantasy come true.

I had often dreamed of being able to cook in a restaurant kitchen, but the first time I went into the kitchen to help Steve I felt like Alice after she swallowed the "drink me" liquid and became tiny. Everything was huge and heavy. Though I am not a short woman, I had to rise on tiptoe to see over the top of the soup pot, use both hands and all my brawn to carry the cans of tomatoes we used for the gazpacho, massage my weary muscles after stirring the boeuf bourguignon, which contained twenty pounds of meat. But I discovered the most dangerous aspect by far of a restaurant kitchen is the need to taste all day long. There is simply no other method for discovering if the gâteau has enough cream, the escargot butter sufficient brandy or the gazpacho plenty of spice.

One honest look at myself in the mirror only weeks after I moved to Orpheus confirmed my worst suspicions. I had, indeed, gained weight. Something had to be done quickly, I decided, and I joined a dance class.

We called ourselves the "Over-Thirty-fives," and we met every Sunday afternoon in a nearby studio. Our instructor made no allowance for age, exercising us as ruthlessly as a drill sergeant with a group of rookies.

There were fourteen in the class, which included Steffi, Margaret Gibson, Carol Mailer and myself. Margaret, as a girl, had been an aspiring dancer and the model for "Gittel" in her husband Bill's play *Two for the Seesaw*. She is a small bundle of dynamite who set the energetic and exhausting pace of the class that first Sunday.

I suggested that the entire group come back to Orpheus for a drink after class. The majority did. The next Sunday more came, joined by husbands and friends. By the third Sunday the inn became the "meeting place" and Carol Mailer insisted that since we were an inn, we must charge or no one would feel free to continue coming. From that beginning was born "Le Club Dimanche." The inn, thereafter, except for the Tanglewood season, was closed to the public on Sunday nights.

Carol Mailer is one of the most beautiful women I have ever known, tall, with well-chiseled bones and enormous black eyes which are deep and compassionate. She also possesses a full-throated, warm, blues-singing voice. As Carol Stevens she had made recordings and sung in clubs, but she had been inactive for a number of years. At the weekly sessions of Le Club Dimanche she sang again. One day as Steve and I sat with Norman and Carol over a bottle of Pott's rum, we discussed the idea of Carol Stevens singing on Friday nights at Orpheus.

Carol's eloquent eyes grew enormous with expectation.

She had very little time for herself. The Mailer house was filled with the frenetic activity that life with a celebrity creates. Carol also had to organize a household, often consisting of Norman's six children from four previous marriages; their own three-year-old, Maggie; Carol's grown son, David; Norman's mother; and a long list of guests.

We all decided that the sooner she began singing at the inn the better. Carol worked hard on her repertoire while Steve advertised that Miss Carol Stevens was to open in cabaret at Orpheus Ascending two weeks from that Friday.

We pushed the piano back to give Carol a stage area. Her entrance, however, had to be from the swinging kitchen door, her exit through the lounge, between the guests, and her final disappearance into the public telephone booth beneath the stairs.

Opening night in she swept, wearing a magnificent bright green chiffon gown, yards and yards of flowing fabric attached to glittering rhinestone clips at the shoulders of the dress. The cook and the dishwasher stood by to make sure the door did not swing closed before Carol and cape were out of danger.

The gels had been changed to give a soft blue stage light, and the room beyond was made even darker than usual. Carol stood majestically at the microphone, her dark hair piled into a Grecian crown on her head. Norman sat at one of the window banquettes which offered the best view of Carol. The adjoining banquette was occupied by two couples who were strangers to Orpheus. They had been drinking heavily and were noisy and extremely high-spirited.

Carol began her first number. Norman leaned over and politely asked the man seated closest to him to be quiet. The man ignored him. Norman bristled, drew back, but all the while Carol was singing it was obvious the strangers were straining his tolerance level. Halfway through Carol's third number, the man nearest Norman turned away from his companions and called out, "Is that broad stacked!"

"Be quiet," Norman ordered.

"Sex-y!" the man continued.

With that Norman turned to face the stranger, grabbed him by the ears and in a split moment had butted his own head so hard against the man's head that there was a resounding *craaaaack!* The stranger was holding his head and moaning. Norman had turned back to watch Carol. She was a ghostly sight, unable to conceal the fear in her eyes as she raised the decibel level of her voice.

"That old man nearly cracked my skull," shouted the stranger, pointing to Norman's tousled gray head.

Norman rose to his feet and pushed the table back. "I challenge you to a re-butt," he said.

Carol stopped singing. The two men stepped out into the narrow aisle between tables. Steve came running, pushing himself between them. "The house will buy everyone drinks in the bar," he said, sweating.

I thought, "My God, he'll get hurt standing between those two!" I pushed my chair back, stumbled to my feet, reached up and grabbed Norman's arm. "Remember, Norman," I said inanely, not able to think of anything else, "this isn't just a supper club, it is also my home."

Norman suspended his challenging glance as he turned to me. I held my breath. Carol was behind me. "If you do this, Norman," she said over my shoulder, "I'll never forgive you." She began to cry and I turned and held her against my shoulder.

"We'll go outside," Norman decided, as the stranger let out a string of abusive remarks and curses.

Steffi, Joan Mills and I took Carol upstairs. "Someday," Carol cried, "someone will have a knife. Maybe that crazy man he challenged has one." She was terrified, angry and inconsolable. "Go down and see what's happening," she begged. "It's too quiet. I can't stand it."

78

There was no one in the lounge. I walked into the bar. It was jammed with people. Standing in the center were Norman and the stranger, no longer a stranger, bear-hugging, toasting each other.

"You have a hard head," Norman said admiringly.

"Yours is pretty tough for an old man," admitted Norman's new friend. Steve later explained that the man had met Norman in a re-butt and been able to remain on his feet, thereby gaining Norman's sincere respect.

The local critics didn't come to see Carol until the third Friday, and by then Norman was the epitome of reserve. Eventually, Carol's appearance was given national coverage. *Time* sent a crew and ran a picture of her, captioned "Carol Mailer Sings to Norman." Carol had been billed at Orpheus as Carol Stevens and had worked professionally under that name. I wrote a letter to the editors of *Time* telling them that their magazine was "a male chauvinist organ," but they never printed it.

Steve and I had a front room overlooking the roof of La Verandah. The bathroom, unfortunately, could be reached only by going out into the second-floor hallway. The total lack of privacy was beginning to prove to be the most difficult aspect of my inn life. There were public bathrooms adjoining the bar, but too often, if they were in use, a perfect stranger would wander upstairs and use ours. After a few weekends, when I found lipsticks, colognes and even my chopsticks missing, I had to remove all personal items. This meant having to pack and carry a small overnight bag with me every time I wanted to take a bath. It also meant being plagued by requests and complaints from houseguests on my way to and from the bath.

Guests never thought that Steve and I, as innkeepers, were entitled to much privacy. If they wanted something and knew we were in our room they did not hesitate to knock at the door and enter, without further word. Outrageously early one morning there was a polite tap on the door. Sleepily, Steve called out, "Who is it?"

The door swung wide open. I grabbed the blanket and pulled it up around myself.

"My husband and I," our guest began, "thought we would start out early and see Williamstown. Do you know what time the Clark Museum opens?"

We went out and bought DO NOT DISTURB signs, quickly discovering that they worked for guests but not for innkeepers.

"I'm sorry to disturb you," a guest would now politely begin after throwing open our door.

Steve found an old brass andiron in the basement and every night before we went to bed he pushed it in front of our door. However, that meant that if one of us went to the bathroom in the middle of the night the andiron had to be dragged away from the door, and when we returned, pushed back. Mornings I would awake with sore arm muscles.

There were also social adjustments. I had made many friends in the ten months I lived in the house on Christian Hill, and I was accustomed to entertaining as often as I wished. As innkeepers this sort of open house was an impossibility. Even having a few friends as our guests for dinner presented problems because we were constantly obliged to leave the table when summoned by guests, waiters, the secretary or chef. More difficult yet, it seemed, was the social problem of what to do when a good friend came in as a paying customer. We bought them drinks or sent over wine or a special dessert, but even then, if either of us was near their table when they were presented with the check, there was an instinct to say "Forget it" that had to be overcome if we were to survive financially.

I tried very hard, though, to retain a sense of family. Cathy had a friend visiting from Switzerland who was house-sitting at Christian Hill until a decision could be made as to what to do about the lease. If Cathy came home for the weekend, she stayed at Christian Hill, and I would arrange early dinners for us at Orpheus so that we could eat together without too many interruptions. But there isn't much of an "at home" feeling when you are dining in an empty restaurant with waiters hovering about you setting up tables.

Perhaps the most frustrating restraint was the claustrophobic nature of our lives when the inn was open. If we wanted to be alone it had to be in our bedroom. There was no other area where we could dine, play Scrabble, watch television or simply talk. I began rising early to accompany Steve on his marketing chores so that we could have some private time.

Not only did that one fourteen-by-fourteen-foot bedroom represent our home, it also contained all the private memorabilia and possessions necessary to convert it to a home. My needlepoint pillows weren't safe in the public sitting room, nor were our favorite books or objets d'art. The paintings on the bedroom walls were those we were selling from the gallery. Boxed and stored in the basement were our own china, silver and linens. Abandoned was the free choice of cooking something you might simply be in the mood for.

Yet I had never been happier in my entire life. When Michael was a child I told him that life was like a marvelous book. He had countered with, "What if you don't like the book?" To which I had replied, "Close it and start another."

I had begun a new book, a new life. And no matter what the drawbacks there was a great and constant excitement to it. The important element seemed to be the sharing. We were not young (we were not old either!), and for the first time each of us had found a partner who complemented us perfectly. Nothing cheered me more than to see Steve's handsome face break into a smile or to hear his heavy footsteps nearing the bedroom door. We enjoyed cooking, shopping and entertaining our guests together. We loved each other and we loved being together.

Before Steve and I met I had once flatly stated to Steffi, who

81

was also going through an unpleasant divorce, "No more men."
She had arched an eyebrow and replied, "*Chéri*, you can say
that and I can say that and actually believe it. You know why?
Because we are both Hungarian. But no one else would believe
it for a wink of an eye."

I had moved to the country not for the usual reasons, but
rather to begin a new life in a place without old memories and
old friends. I had succeeded in accomplishing that, though not
as I thought I would. Now I could look at the countryside and
at nature. In California, where I was brought up, the seasons
ran together like the paints in a child's water color. There was
no one morning when you awoke, looked out your window and
suddenly knew it was spring. In London, where I lived for so
many years, the arrival of spring became known when daffodils
appeared on flower carts and the snow melted and the days
were longer and not quite so gray, but the change of season was
mostly a state of mind. You said, "*I must pack away my wool-
ens, fill the house with flowers and walk more.*" But that was
about it. The weather was still damp and raw. The days gray.
Spring was simply a muted winter. On our five acres in the
Berkshires, spring was breathtaking. The brook suddenly
brimmed and bubbled crystal clear, the apple trees snapped
into bloom, wild violets and starflowers sprang up to carpet the
woods, shiny emerald green lawns unrolled from under the
melted snow and the bird feeders were festooned with vivid
plumage.

Doug began to mend the fences and touch up faded shutters
and peeling paint, so that when the bold spring sun brushed
the roof and clapboard, Orpheus seemed newly awakened and
very lovely. I was beginning to feel quite proprietary about the
place. We had one of the best views of the gentle Berkshire
hills with their lavender peaks and soft shoulders. We had a
small wooded area of the finest firs in the country. Our hearths
flamed the best fires. The house itself was a grand and admirable survivor; the winter storms, the lashing rains, had only

smeared the great lady's make-up. She, herself, remained composed, promising—with love—to survive another one hundred and thirty years.

In the entire inn the object I admired most was the old Garland stove. It was constructed of solid cast iron and was approximately sixty years old. Though the star of the kitchen, it was, alas, a most temperamental performer. There was no way to regulate the oven temperature, the flame in the broiler or the heat of the griddle. The oven doors cranked open like the first steps of the *Bride of Frankenstein* and often refused to be shut. One night Rebecca put in a huge baking dish of chicken Mornay and as it bubbled over, a thick trail of sauce oozed to the floor through the bottom of the stove, which had suddenly become a sieve.

The stove had to go, and what a trauma that created. The Garland was a real personality, and we all felt as if a valued fellow worker was being given the sack.

The new stove was the first inn purchase Steve and I made together and we treated it as a special occasion. We took the day off and left Yousef in charge until our planned late-evening return, for we had to travel to Albany where the nearest Garland stove supplier was located. We had a festive lunch on the road and then descended upon the poor dealer, spending long hours studying every inch of every model as though we had to make sure our choice was seaworthy. We went out for coffee with pamphlets and our voluminous notes. We returned an hour later, our decision made, and had the salesman explain once again every feature of the new purchase—a gleaming, black model that closely resembled the old one. Then we went to an elegant Albany restaurant and ordered their best champagne.

We drove back to Stockbridge singing, happy that we had bought a stove together. Suddenly, a terrible thought struck me.

"Darling, pull over to the side of the road," I said, in a voice that I prayed did not sound too alarming.

Steve, convinced I was ill from the champagne, stopped the car. "You look green," he said tenderly. "Shall we take a little walk in the fresh air?"

"No, I just wanted to avoid an accident," I replied.

"Why should we have an accident? The car is in great condition, there is no traffic, and see"—he held his hand up —"steady as they come."

"I just had this disturbing thought," I began as carefully as I could, "and I didn't want to give you a heart attack. I mean . . . we just gave that firm a check for *two thousand one hundred and forty-three dollars and fifty-six cents,* right?"

"Right."

"For a brand-new, glorious, divine stove—right?"

"Right!"

"Darling . . ."

"Ummm?"

"How are we going to get the old one out?"

It took three days, six workers and an additional *thirteen hundred dollars.* First of all, the old stove was molded from one solid, massive block of iron. Furthermore, the house no longer had a doorway wide enough for it to pass through. The two doors to the present kitchen were so narrow that a waiter could just squeeze by.

The wall and doorway leading to the back kitchen had to come down, and the rear doorway was widened. After the old stove was moved outside it had to be lifted on a truck to be hauled away. Everyone went out back to watch, as if we were mourners and the old black stove an iron casket on its way to its final resting place—a scrap-metal yard in Housatonic. But as the four men we had hired hoisted the stove onto the dolly, the sudden weight caused the wheels to spin, and the dolly,— topped by the stove, zoomed forward. It sped downhill, finally halting and depositing its cargo at the foot of two giant aged elms behind the kitchen. To accomplish the original plan the stove would have to go back on the dolly and the dolly and stove would have to be pushed uphill over the muddy grounds to the truck. But the stove was now sunk up to its burners in mud. Steve, unable to bear any more, told them to leave it where it was, partially buried, and the next day Doug planted some vines that would cover the old Garland in its last repose.

Sharing also meant worrying together about the financial problems of the inn. Even I, inept bookkeeper that I am, could see that we were still heavily in the red. But I was as much an optimist as Steve, and it seemed to me only a matter of time before the inn would be a financial as well as a critical success.

We were beginning to attract some of the local people for dinner, and by late spring the rooms were about 80 percent occupied on weekends. Reviews appeared in major travel books and magazines—and Steve was riding high.

"We're a smash hit, baby!" he crowed as he animatedly read me a review that appeared in *Lover's Guide to America:* "Orpheus and Eros and Bacchus—they're all ascendant here, a jovial trio who make this a welcome newcomer, because there's never been anything around the Berkshires with quite the same casual sophistication, the same Broadway-weekending-in-the-Berkshires atmosphere. The OA's guest list includes the Norman Mailers, Leonard Bernstein, and members of the Boston Symphony who often drop by for dinner after their concerts."

Steve let out a small cheer before continuing: "Orpheus Ascending gets its unusual ambiance from its owner, Stephen Citron, a pianist/composer who was once Piaf's accompanist. While he lived in the land of *haute cuisine,* he learned to play pots and pans as well as piano, and when he returned to this country he bought a Christmas-tree farm and modulated it into a French-style country inn with a piano bar, where Citron plays Citron, except when his show biz friends decide to entertain *him.*"

There were other good reviews. *New York* magazine printed

a story entitled "A Room at the Inn," which began: "Classic Eighteen Forty-seven Colonial on the outside, Orpheus inside is pure supper-club-modern—black walls plastered with Carnegie Hall posters, chrome chairs, black marble bar. The menu, too, is unorthodox. Old favorites like boeuf bourguignon are offered along with such inventions as pork chops marinated in sherry and ham with raspberries. The bread is super and the pâté is so good it's hard to believe."

Even the conservative *Guide to the Recommended Country Inns of New England* reported: "Off-beat, charming, gracious, intriguing, all these words can only begin to apply to Orpheus Ascending. . . . The food is truly outstanding, and the bedrooms with the French Provincial fabric-hung walls will make you feel you have found a true French country inn."

Steve and I agreed that Orpheus was truly ascending, but Paul Josephson, our accountant, was not nearly so encouraging. One day he called from New York to say he was coming to Stockbridge to go over the books and that we should prepare everything in chronological order.

After the last Le Club Dimanche member departed on Sunday night we dragged boxes from the gallery closet and began to sort. By Tuesday the gallery rug was a checkerboard of piles; Massachusetts forms, federal forms, Stockbridge forms, canceled checks and room receipts were everywhere.

Paul was a serious young man who had been coping for some time with Steve's incomprehensible personal records, and he did not appear surprised when he saw what awaited him in the gallery. By early afternoon the rug was clear and the desk piled high with neatly indexed folders. Steve poked his head in. "Surprised you, didn't I?" He grinned. "Everything was ready for you."

"Where are the bar tabs and the restaurant checks?" Paul barked back at him.

"You have them."

"Not all of them. Otherwise your figures are way off."

We went on a search. There were tabs behind the bar, on the rack in the kitchen, in the utility drawers and under the cash register. "Why don't you get one big spindle and put everything on it?" Paul grumbled.

"I bought several spindles, but I ended up spearing recipes and messages on them," Steve explained.

He threw up his hands. "I'll have to stay over. I'll never finish tonight."

"Good. We can talk about our plans for this season, then."

He looked up nervously and adjusted his glasses. "What plans?" he asked.

Steve went around the desk, and pushing the stack to one side, sat down on the edge. "First of all," he began excitedly, "I'm going to get the pool in operating condition. We won't be like the Wayside Inn. They advertise 'pool' and all they have is a pool table in the lounge. No, we have to have a fantastic pool! That means a new filter system and a new floor. We'll have to repave the poolside, fence the area and put up one of those electronic things that gets rid of all the bugs. And we need a poolhouse so that our guests won't drip through the inn to get to their rooms. I think I'd like some French-style wrought-iron furniture—red, white and blue tables and lounges and some large umbrellas so we can serve lunch and cocktails outside all day. And we need a proper diving board."

"You can't encumber yourself with more debts," Paul said, his nose twitching. "From the figures so far it looks to me like you're operating at a loss."

"Well, it's only been a year and we had all the opening expenses. This place was a ruin when I came in," Steve explained.

"It will be a fiasco if you don't pull in your belt," Paul warned.

"I'll get you a drink. Your problem is that you don't know how to relax," Steve told him. "Orpheus is closed tonight, so we'll have dinner at one of the local restaurants. It will be easier

87

for you to understand what I've accomplished here if you dine at the competition."

The three of us went to dinner. "Look at this thimble of Scotch," Steve complained, holding up the drink he had just been served.

"It's better business than the three ounces of Scotch you serve at Orpheus for which you charge the same amount," Paul said.

"I hate stingy drinks. And anyway, we're building a reputation."

"You know about the twenty-five percent rule?" Paul asked.

"What twenty-five percent rule?"

"Your food costs are supposed to come to twenty-five percent of your menu price," Paul explained. "It is a standard and basic formula for restaurant operation. And if you had asked my advice last year before you printed your menus, Steve, I would have guided you." He went on, getting more excited. "Take for instance your filet mignon, which you pay for by the ounce. The ounce, for God's sake! One eight-ounce steak is costing you two dollars and sixty-five cents. How about the sauce?"

"We just use a little brandy and calvados," I explained.

"You pay thirty cents an ounce for calvados. What kind of brandy do you use?"

"Courvoisier," Steve said.

"You cook with Courvoisier?"

"The cheaper brands give a bitter taste," Steve explained.

"Courvoisier is thirty-five cents an ounce." Paul took out a small book and a pen. "What else is in the sauce?"

"Some butter, shallots, a little sour cream."

"Fifteen cents minimum. And what goes with it?"

"Salad, pommes de terre allumettes and a fresh vegetable," I added.

"I studied your invoices. You use three or four very expensive varieties of greens for your salad," Paul accused.

"Iceberg lettuce is an abomination," Steve bridled.

"It's also cheaper. And can't you get carrots, or turnips, or squash for your fresh vegetable instead of asparagus, broccoli and artichokes?"

"Of course I can get them, but I prefer the others," Steve said.

"Steve, look at these figures." Paul shoved his book beneath Steve's nose. "You charge five fifty for a meal that costs you over four dollars and that does not take into consideration linens, service, mortgages, heating, electricity, soap, water . . ."

"And you haven't remembered that I am building, *building*, Paul. When I have more of a reputation I can charge more, but I refuse to give my guests less than the best." Our steaks had just been served and Steve watched me cutting mine. "Look at Anne," he said. "At Orpheus you can cut the filet with a spoon. Here you can't even cut it with a knife!"

"Yeah," said Paul, "but I assure you the guy who runs this place doesn't pay for his meat by the ounce."

By noon the next day Paul had all the figures together. He came into the bar where I sat while Steve was on the telephone. Paul waited impatiently.

"What did the contractor say?" I asked Steve.

"He can tear down the wall without any problem."

"You are not planning to tear down walls," Paul wailed. "You are not!"

"Of course we are. We have to break through the window wall in our room. It leads out onto the roof over La Verandah and will make a fantastic terrace. We're going to floor it in redwood and put up a large red, white and blue striped awning that will extend the full width of the building. Anne can write there, Lex can play there."

"Steve," Paul said, like a funeral director quoting figures to the family of the deceased, "you lost *fourteen thousand two hundred and sixteen dollars and fifty-eight cents* in your first year of operation."

"That's not bad," Steve answered. "For the first year, that's not bad at all. With the pool, and if we air-condition the third floor so that we can rent those rooms, too, and if we add a full breakfast—omelettes aux choix—we can raise our prices and accommodate more people."

"Steve, we're old friends. Remember when you wanted to lease a larger studio at Carnegie . . ."

"It was a mistake that I didn't, Paul. A big mistake. The trouble with you—and believe me, Paul, I say this because I love you—the trouble with you is that you don't see far enough ahead. You read our reviews. We'll *triple* our business this summer. I'll talk to the bank. I'm sure they'll give me a larger home-improvement loan. We're a success, Paul. Hell! We have to act like one."

Construction began. I had convinced Steve that the piano could not remain in the corner by the door where the noise and traffic from the kitchen competed with his music. To correct this meant pulling down the partition that separated the two areas of the lounge.

This work and the other construction continued at a dizzying pace on Mondays through Thursdays, when the inn was closed to the public. Friday mornings were madness—preparing for the weekend guests, sweeping away sawdust, touching up scraped spots with quick-drying paint, cleaning workmen's tracks from carpet and floors. Monday through Wednesday I remained in charge while Steve went into New York to conduct his classes. When I finally decided to close the house on Christian Hill, I brought the poodles over for company because, after the dozens of workmen, the constant barrage of electric saws and the banging of hammers, nights without Steve at Orpheus were awesome. One cannot imagine how dispiriting it is to go into a restaurant kitchen for a cup of coffee and be confronted by ten-gallon pots gleaming and empty, a mammoth stove clear and cold, open shelves stacked with hundreds of clean dishes and a coffee-maker unable to brew less than twenty cups.

Eating alone amidst so many empty tables and sixty vacant chairs in a room lighted by ten-watt bulbs was equally intimidating. It was also somewhat uncomfortable to hear the same sounds from the third floor that made the dogs run for the attic stairway and then sit yowling. Mice most probably, I reasoned. But then I am not easy about mice. The ghost of an Indian princess waiting behind the door seemed less disquieting.

Invariably, having settled myself in bed, the dogs at the foot, downstairs lights extinguished, a car would grind up the driveway and someone would pound on the door. I wouldn't answer, but soon someone would call from under the window, "Hey, up there! Open up! We need a room." Or sometimes the demand was for a telephone or a pack of cigarettes.

"We're closed," I would shout down in as masculine a voice as I could manage. I would also nudge the poodles, hoping they would bark. They never did, obviously saving their canine hostility for mice. The poodles, who were now living at Orpheus, presented a new complication.

"If they are going to be inn dogs," Steve decreed, "they will have to learn to *be* inn dogs."

This entailed keeping them out of all the downstairs areas except for the sitting room and gallery. Unfortunately, both of the poodles—Biba, the mother, and Krissy, her daughter— suffered from severe claustrophobia. They would become frantic if they happened to be locked into a room, or persistent— clawing at woodwork and rugs—if locked out. Because of this, Cathy and I had never left the dogs locked in any area of the house.

I decided to leave our bedroom door open but close the door leading from the hallway to the front staircase, giving Biba and Krissy a less confined feeling while at the same time prohibiting

91

them from following me into the dining lounge.

Carol was then singing every Friday night, and the night I left the dogs alone for the first time Orpheus was crowded to capacity. I sat at a circular table nearest the piano with Norman, his mother and several of the Mailer children. As Carol sang, suddenly there was the sound of scratching at the service door behind her.

Norman looked puzzled, the kids tittered, but Carol continued like a true professional. Then there was a *yip*, followed by a *yap-yap*. I edged my chair out as carefully as I could and stole out of the room, then I dashed upstairs and threw open the hallway door. Tails wagging, the dogs ran back up the service stairs to greet me. I had no alternative but to remain in our room with them for the remainder of the evening.

"They have to learn," Steve announced the next morning. "Tonight lock them in our room."

"But they'll carry on terribly," I protested.

"You won't hear them from downstairs and eventually they'll give up," he reasoned.

I gave each dog a huge roast beef bone just before I went down to the lounge. Steve began his set late in the evening, but midway through a Rodgers and Hart love song there was a tremendous crash from above. From the piano, Steve signaled me to investigate, and with Yousef leading the way, I went upstairs.

Silence.

"It sounded like broken glass. Maybe someone threw a rock through a window as a warning or a reprisal," Yousef said.

"In Stockbridge?" I asked.

"There is great unrest in the working classes," Yousef announced.

I went directly to our bedroom door. As I opened it, I heard scraping and then the sound of dogs whimpering. Broken bits of mirror were scattered everywhere and from beneath the bed two pairs of terrified eyes stared out at us. The fringe of the bedspread covered their top knots and hid their ears, so that they looked like two little old ladies in babushkas. Apparently they had scratched at the base of the door until the full-length mirror hanging there came crashing down.

The next weekend Steve decided it was better to take our chances with the board of health than with the havoc the dogs could create. We brought them down to the lounge where they sat on any welcoming lap and curled up under the piano when Steve sat down to play. After that, whenever the health officer came around, the dogs were instantly whisked up to our room, where I would remain with them until all was clear again.

I was always apprehensive about rodents and the larger, wilder country creatures and the dogs gave me a sense of protection, for though they welcomed strangers they were extremely hostile to other animals. One week when Steve was in New York, one of his Parisian cousins came to visit. Solange was the first member of Steve's family I had met. She was warm, intelligent and attractive and I liked her immediately. Happily for me, her English was better than my French. We conversed late into the night and then she accompanied me as I turned off all the lights and locked the doors.

"It is quite beeg in 'ere and quite dark out *there*, eh Ann-ie?" she said nervously.

"Are you frightened, Solange?" I asked.

"No, no, no."

We started up to our rooms.

"You 'ave a friendly neighbor, per'aps?"

"I hardly know our neighbors, Solange. But look, we'll both keep our bedroom doors open. Okay?"

The corridor stretched long and dark before us. "Okay," Solange agreed.

I was exhausted and fell quickly to sleep only to be awakened some time later by a sound which I decided was an animal chewing on a bone. I sat there paralyzed with fear. Dinner had not provided any bones that Biba or Krissy could have taken

93

from the garbage, and animals in the country could be wild bears, skunks or foxes. I remained stiff and unmoving a 'few moments, accustoming my eyes to the dark, not wanting to turn on a light that might attract the beast. Finally I glanced nervously around the room.

Krissy was sleeping on the foot of the bed, not even alerted, but Biba was missing. "Oh, Lord," I thought, "whatever species of wild beast is out in the hallway it is devouring little Biba!"

I slipped from the bed as soundlessly as I could, and as I passed the fireplace on my way to the hall, I grabbed the poker. Then I stood poised for a moment in the doorway, poker raised to defend the small dog. Moonlight shone brightly through the hallway's north window.

There was Biba, unharmed, gnawing away at what looked like—indeed was—a set of false teeth.

"Biba," I screamed, "drop those!" I ran to dislodge them from her jaws with the tip of the poker.

Solange appeared in her doorway.

"It's okay, Solange," I assured her. "It's not a wild animal, only Biba and . . ." I stopped suddenly, gasping. "Solange! Oh-my-God! They're not yours, are they?"

They were the only set she owned. I grabbed the gnawed teeth and handed them to her, assuring her that Berkshire County had fantastic dentists and we would see one that very morning—*early.*

When Solange came down to breakfast, the teeth were in place, though the two front ones were missing and the gums were a mushy pink mess. I poured her coffee and got up to boil some eggs when Biba jumped onto Solange's lap and, growling, snapped at her mouth.

"Down!" I commanded. Biba minded, but then stood on the side of Solange's chair, still growling. "She thinks you have her bone," I said numbly, but as I ran from the room Solange roared with laughter.

"Ann-ie!" she called after me. "All I ask is that you hide me until my new teeth are ready."

The loveliest time at Orpheus was just before season. The weather was clear and bright, the sky a delphinium blue and the hills a complex abstract of evergreen. Every morning I would pick armfuls of blossoms. The inn smelled like a florist's shop and looked as though a wedding was in progress. We bought seed catalogs and visited all the local nurseries. La Verandah was crowded with seedlings and plants and pots and tools, because we soon learned that most of what we had bought could not be planted until after the late spring and early summer New England frosts.

The accountant's forebodings hadn't daunted Steve, and with Orpheus looking splendid in its early summer frippery— lilac and pink magnolia dipping over its eaves, the sun warm and buttery on its timbers and beams—we were both optimistic about our first full season together. Steve decided to complete the pool and the upstairs terrace, install air conditioning on the third floor and renovate our room so that the bathroom could be entered without going into the hallway. I was helping with all the secretarial work. Each day brought in new summer reservation deposits. Feeling reassured, Steve went to the bank and took a loan of $10,000 for ninety days to cover the cost of all the improvements. He returned home, gloating, and reported, "The bank also thinks our summer reservations warrant a forward approach."

But when we called Paul to report this to him, he warned, "Put five thousand away in case you run into trouble midseason."

The work already contracted made that impossible. What Steve did instead was set aside $1,000 to enlarge our advertising budget. We had found that the more sophisticated outlets, such as *New York* magazine, brought us the best results. We ran a weekly ad that read: "Your French Connection in the

Berkshires. Only thirteen beds. Orpheus Ascending, Route 7, Stockbridge. 413-298-4700."

In early June, workmen swarmed over our bedroom. The pool men drained the swimming pool, and around it the fence people sank holes among the bushes and the trees, since Steve had insisted that the fence be concealed by foliage. The cost had been considerably higher than anticipated, but he felt the guests would be more relaxed, less restrained, with the chain fencing hidden from view and, perhaps, would order more drinks.

When the work was finally complete, Mr. Moritz, the pool builder, attached the garden hose to the well spigot. He ceremoniously turned the handle, and then with the greatest insouciance, threw the nozzle into the newly tiled and painted pool. Cool crystal water gushed forth. We stepped closer to the edge and watched the tiny trickle make spaghetti-thin streaks on the wet tile at the bottom.

Mr. Moritz was a tall, lean man not given to many words. "It should take about a week to fill," he said.

"A week!" Steve complained. "Can't we put more force behind the water?"

"Any faster, an' you might deplete the well," Mr. Moritz warned.

"It still shouldn't take a week if it runs twenty-four hours a day," Steve insisted.

"Shut it off at night or I won't be responsible. Anything happens to the valve and it would be ruined before you discovered it in the morning," Mr. Moritz said, handing Steve a bill. "This here's for labor. All the hours are listed. I'll send one for the materials and chemicals when I get back to the office." He hopped into his truck cab as though he were mounting a horse. "Like I said," he called down, "I won't be responsible for any foolhardy impatience."

We returned to the pool. Steve's eyes were shining with

excitement. I leaned close and whispered to him, "It means a lot to you, doesn't it?"

"You understand," he replied. "I knew you would. A pool is important to a man who has grown up on concrete city streets. The only pool I knew during the long, hot summers was the block fire hydrant."

The day was ending. The sky went from blue to rose to deep magenta.

"Hey, next week we can have our first swim in our own pool," Steve crowed. "And damned if we can't skinny dip if we want to! How about that?"

"I know this will come as a great shock," I replied, "I mean my being brought up in California where rumor has it there's a pool in every backyard, and the sun shines all the time—but I can't swim. In fact, I'm terrified of water."

Steve looked at me incredulously. "I'll teach you," he decided. You'll overcome any fear you ever had. And if you don't," he added, laughing, "hell! you can wade in the altogether and float in my arms."

We sat down at the edge and dangled our legs over the hard cement. "Happy?" he asked.

"Delirious," I replied.

"Don't move," he said and jumped up. "I'll be right back."

He returned with two martinis, and we sat there drinking and watching the pool fill at an incredibly slow rate until the mosquitoes drove us inside.

The next day Steve had a gadget installed beside the poolhouse that looked like a tall pole with grillwork on top. It was an electronic machine that drew bugs to it and then electrocuted them. Even in the kitchen I could hear the constant *sssst!* which meant another bug was being killed. It was like living next to the death house at San Quentin.

"You'll have to turn off that machine," I insisted. "Or I'll be traumatized in no time."

97

"You'll get used to it," Steve replied.

But I never did and by the end of the week the electronic executioner was disconnected.

During that week I was puzzled that the pool was filling much more quickly than Mr. Moritz said it would. It turned out Steve had paid Doug double time to work nights so that the water flow could be continuous. On the fourth day the pool was filled, and Steve invited the staff to drink champagne and go for an afternoon swim. Only Mrs. Gretchner refused, taking a rather dim view of the whole frivolous occasion.

The bedroom terrace was also a great success. Ceiling-to-floor glass doors opened onto it, giving us a magnificent view of the Berkshire Hills and flooding our bedroom with morning sun. The terrace was a perfect place to write. Voices would waft up from below, but they formed only a soft background buzz to my new private retreat. Adding to the privacy of the bedroom was the new entrance directly into the bathroom from our room. Back went the baskets of lipsticks, make-up and chopsticks! Up went the hooks for robes and clothes.

The atmosphere of Orpheus was markedly different from that of any other restaurant in the Berkshires. In fact, I had experienced something similar only at Chasen's Restaurant in Beverly Hills, California, in the 1930s.

Dave Chasen, who had been a fairly successful vaudevillian, was my uncle. When I was about three and the depression was at its worst, my father drove seven of us across country in an old La Salle touring car. Uncle Dave was already in Hollywood, and the family hoped that he would be able to "open doors" for the rest of us. Unfortunately, in signing Uncle Dave, Hollywood had overlooked the fact that he was a mime. It was a rather serious oversight because he had been signed for a speaking role. That was the end of his film career, but as my Aunt Theo, his first wife, liked to cook, and as they had rented a house large enough for gatherings, no one went hungry.

Besides a hungry group of out-of-work relatives, Uncle Dave also had a hungry troupe of out-of-work vaudevillian friends. Aunt Theo fed everyone and afterward there was always spontaneous entertainment. There were, as well, friends who were not out of work, like Ruby Keeler and Al Jolson, W. C. Fields and comedian Joe Penner. The entertainment would go on until the wee hours, and though I was generally put to sleep in the bedroom, I would drag my blanket into the doorway, and huddled up, listen to the singing and clowning from the front room.

Weekend nights at Orpheus carried me back to those years, for we attracted all the promising talent in the area. They would come for a drink and soon edge their way over to Steve at the piano. Steve's students came, as did many performers with whom he had worked in clubs. All of them would do a "turn" before the evening's end. Some nights there were so many entertainers that their time had to be limited so that everyone could perform. It was joyous, excellent and mostly impromptu. There was no "stage" except for the few inches that separated the piano from the nearest tables. Performers and audience were crammed together in one group, all members of a private party at a public place. Strangers would join us, but shortly they would talk to the people at the next table and often they, too, would join in singing or commenting.

No matter how exhausted I was—rising early to shop with Steve, writing a minimum of six hours a day, then helping him in the chores of readying Orpheus for the evening—I found I could not go up to bed while the music continued downstairs. I would curl myself in the corner of the window banquette, much as I had done in the doorway at Uncle Dave's, and listen until the last note was struck on the piano.

Steve hired a large staff and even I was concerned at the expenditure. "We've booked almost all the rooms for the main concert weekends," he assured me, "and it's only June. With the pool and all the advertising we can't help doubling our business."

The next day he hired a secretary. Her name was Cornelia Potts. Cornelia had worked for the previous seven years at a local girls' convent school and came with impeccable and glowing references. She explained that since she was presently going through a divorce the atmosphere in the convent had proved difficult.

Cornelia turned out to be remarkable. Slender and frail-looking, always dressed in blouses with Peter Pan collars buttoned to the neck no matter how warm the day, she worked nonstop from arrival until departure. She had a mania for cleanliness, and within three days Steve's desk was cleared, the typewriter gleaming, the telephone shining like black patent leather, the contents of all the boxes in the gallery closet filed, the letters caught up and the cloakroom neatly arranged. She brushed the dogs every day, took the curtains home to wash and iron, picked all the dandelions from our lawn for dandelion wine, tended her own house, took care of two teenage daughters and sewed every stitch of clothing she wore. Her industry exhausted me and her compulsive cleanliness sent me scurrying upstairs to tidy my closets and drawers and stack all the papers neatly on my desk.

Cornelia typed as if she'd been programmed by a computer and took dictation at an alarming speed. Steve had never had a personal secretary before, and for the first few days he was dictating letters to every company and every old friend he could think of. "A secretary is not a toy," I reminded him.

But Cornelia's greatest attribute was her total "unflappability." According to Cornelia, there was never a crisis—there were *events.* A flood in the basement was given no more emphasis than a canceled reservation or a dissatisfied customer. She treated all events with efficiency and detachment.

One morning when Steve had gone into town she tapped

gently on our door. She stood barefoot and dripping in the hallway; her brown hair, which was always pinned back neatly from her face, hung in limp wet hanks on her damp forehead. She held a pair of muddied shoes in her hand.

"My God, Cornelia, what happened?" I ran to fetch some towels, calling back, "Come inside and close the door."

She looked better wet than she did dry. I had never noticed before her shapely figure, and her hair looked infinitely better surrounding her face than when it was pulled back. She stood shivering on the tile hearth so as not to stain the rug while I wrapped a bath towel about her. "What happened?" I repeated.

"It's nothing, nothing at all," she replied calmly, as though she were standing in my room dry, impeccable and poised to take dictation.

"It had to be *something,*" I insisted. "You're soaked to the bone."

"Oh, dear," she sighed. "No one called the fire department back."

"The fire department?" I queried inanely.

There was, indeed, the sound of approaching sirens.

"Why is the fire department here?" I cried, having visions of the inn in flames while Cornelia was drying herself. The engines ground to a stop toward the rear of the house. I didn't know what to do. Should we run out onto the terrace and scream or chance opening the hallway door? I had images of flaming corridors and smoke-filled rooms.

"Shall I begin at the beginning?" Cornelia asked.

"Cornelia, hurry!" I shouted.

"Well, I was parking my car in the back, and as I got out I thought I smelled something burning, so I went to investigate. I have a very strong sense of smell. It's one of the things I pride myself on."

"Cornelia!"

"It turned out to be the rear of the poolhouse. Flames were

101

just beginning to snap. I ran to the kitchen door and shouted to Mrs. Gretchner to call the Stockbridge Fire Brigade and then I connected the garden hose. I found I could get a more powerful spray standing back, but I misjudged my distance and I fell into the pool."

"The fire, Cornelia," I reminded her. "Is it under control?"

"Doug came down and put it out with some chemicals, but we did forget to call the fire department back. Do you think I should write them a letter of apology?"

I loaned Cornelia some dry clothes and shoes. Ten minutes later she was busy at the typewriter, not a hair out of place, and I had collapsed on the terrace chaise with an extremely early vodka and tonic. We never discovered how the fire started. Fortunately we carried fire insurance and the damage was repairable before season.

The first Tanglewood concert turns the quiet country main street of Stockbridge into a madhouse. It often took twenty minutes just to progress from one end of the block to the other. Though I knew this, I was still unprepared for the effect on Orpheus. Milling crowds not only stormed our driveway but took up every inch of breathing space inside. I was now thankful that Steve had had the foresight to hire enough staff.

Still, the arrival of the season kept us in a state of constant crisis. The first night we depleted our supply of linen napkins just before the concert crowds descended upon us. We had to wash and dry several loads at accelerated cycles with the kitchen already overcrowded with staff, food and service plates. The next night we ran out of coffee and Steve dashed over to the all-night market. One evening the table candles had not been delivered as promised and the all-night market didn't carry candles. There were only two small ten-watt fixtures in the Orpheus lounge. Atmosphere was one thing, but without candles it was impossible to see. "Call Cornelia," Steve ordered. In five minutes she was there with several boxes of church votive candles.

In spite of all the crises, we were developing a clientele and a reputation among the Tanglewood concertgoers. One evening a very attractive young woman came in with a date. "I hear you have super pâté," she said, "and escargots." She turned to her companion. "You should positively try the escargots, Harry," she urged him.

"We put brandy in our butter," Steve confided.

"I'll have the pâté; you have the escargots. Okay, Harry?"

"Fine, just fine," Harry agreed.

When the food arrived, Harry sat looking down at his escargots, clutching the snail holder and fork in a desperate manner, a look of panic on his face.

"The pâté's *super*," the young lady drawled. "How are the escargots, Harry?"

They were bubbling on the plate below him, the scent of garlic butter reaching us at a nearby table. Suddenly Harry grasped an escargot with a holder, using it like a nutcracker. Butter flew everywhere but the shell did not split. His dinner date stared at him, unbelievingly. With great aplomb Steve reached over and grabbed the holder from the man's hand. "I'm not sure this escargot butter is seasoned well," he said coolly. "We have a new chef. Forgive me. I'll try one and then replace it." With that he took his fork and extracted and ate the snail as Harry watched him carefully.

The next night Harry returned. This time with another girl. I greeted them and had the maître d' show them to a table. "They have the most marvelous escargots here," Harry told the girl. "They put brandy in the butter."

We were honored to serve many of the Tanglewood guest artists. One night Philippe Entremont, the great concert pianist, sat at our piano and played exquisite Debussy. The guests sat with their forks frozen in midair, and the waiters stood immobile, trays on their shoulders, like figures in Madame Tussaud's Waxworks. At moments like that, Orpheus seemed like a *salon* and I knew Steve felt transformed from sal*oon* keeper to sal*on*keeper. Leonard Bernstein came by frequently, sometimes wearing a voluminous black cape. He would stand in the doorway of the lounge looking like Mandrake the Magician. With a wide, sweeping gesture, he would raise his arm to greet Steve at the piano, as if to make Steve, the piano, the diners and the inn part of a disappearing act.

Seiji Ozawa spent one afternoon on the front terrace working on the score of a concert he was giving. And often members of the orchestra would stop by after a concert and give Orpheus late diners a concert of their own.

Carol was not singing during the summer, but she and Norman often dined with us. We did everything possible to protect Norman—seating him in a far corner, his back to the other diners, stopping anyone who looked as if he or she might approach him. Norman was famous for his hand wrestling, and young men, treating him like the best gun in the West, were invariably compelled to challenge him. And young women often accused him of being a male chauvinist pig.

Finding time to be alone was no simple task. The upstairs terrace was our only refuge, but the intercom rang madly, with reports of a crisis in the kitchen, bar, lounge or parking lot. Still, this barrage of problems, the constant pressures, the all-involving and claustrophobic nature of our lives, seemed to bring us closer than we had even been before season. Steve and I shared all the problems, and indeed, if we had not been able to do that, I don't think we could have made it from one day to the next.

One of the personal problems we had was how to present our unmarried status to our guests. At the start of season we were firmly convinced that we should be straightforward. This created an awkward situation in introducing and referring to each other. There is no accepted name for the person with whom you live, unmarried. We rejected "lover," "love," "beloved," "my constant companion," "my friend." Steve suggested he call me his "lady," but I, in turn, said I could never refer to him as "my man," "my lord" or "my liege." We never did and never have solved that problem. It hasn't been a serious social encumbrance in private life, but it produced difficult and embarrassing moments at the inn.

The first weekend of the season, a couple, the Woods, were booked into the room that adjoined ours. It was a lovely room with a double bed and both Bernie and his wife, Lillian, loved it. They had driven all the way from Pittsburgh, and after the complimentary first cocktail we served our arriving guests, Bernie went up to nap before dinner. He was still sleeping by nine o'clock, and Lillian—a slim, nervous lady with a laugh that sounded like a horse's snort—called to me as I went down the stairs.

She was dressed in a stylish cocktail dress and had a white satin evening envelope clasped in her hand. "Mrs. Citron, can I have a word with you?" she managed uneasily, looking around to make sure we were alone.

"Is everything all right?" I asked, playing the innkeeper and choosing to ignore the "Mrs. Citron" in view of her obvious disturbance.

"Well, Bernie is sound asleep and I am afraid I will have to have dinner alone," she said.

It was apparent that Lillian Wood had never dined in a restaurant by herself and did not know what she should do. "Would you like to sit with me?" I offered. "Perhaps Steve can join us for a drink."

"Are you sure I won't intrude?"

"Of course not," I assured her. We had set up tables in the gallery to help relieve the congestion and I selected one for us there.

"This is very kind of you, Mr. Citron," she said, as Steve sat down. "Your wife has been nice enough to ask me to sit with you. I hope that's all right."

"We're not married," I corrected. "My name is Anne Edwards." Steve smiled at me and reached for my hand under the table.

The woman looked right past me as though I had not spoken. "Bernie worked especially hard this week. I guess he's just exhausted. Goodness! Most of the time, when we are on vacation, he is the first one down for dinner." She turned to me, smiling diffidently. "I hope you will forgive him, Mrs. Citron, for inflicting me on you this way."

"Well, Lillian," I began. "May I call you Lillian?"

"Please do."

"Well, Lillian, we like to get to know our guests and this is a perfect opportunity. But I am not Mrs. Citron. Please call me Anne. That's a lot more friendly anyway," I said.

Lillian grew pale. Her hand fluttered as she put her napkin in her lap. Steve ordered drinks. "Lillian, what shall it be?" he asked.

"A sherry, please," she mumbled, and then glanced nervously away.

No sooner had the drinks arrived than she knocked over her sherry. "Oh, dear," she cried, jumping to her feet, "I've stained my clutch!"

Steve stared up at her quite uncomprehendingly.

"We have a good local cleaner," I said. "I'm sure the spot on your purse will come out."

She was standing panic-stricken, a frightened colt not knowing which way to bolt. "Lillian, does it make you uneasy that we're not married?" I asked frankly.

"Yes, yes, it does," she replied.

"In this day and age?" Steve asked with dismay.

"Well, we're in adjoining rooms and . . ." She was quite incapable of continuing.

"Why don't you two ladies move into the lounge," Steve suggested. "I'm about to do my first set."

Lillian followed. She listened politely to the music, ordered her dinner, picked at it and then, as soon as she finished, excused herself. The next day Bernie apologetically requested another room.

From that time we never forced the issue of our status. I was introduced by Steve or Cornelia to guests as Anne Edwards, and Steve referred to me as Anne or Annie. Occasionally he would say, "This is the woman I love," making me feel like the Duchess of Windsor. But to refer to him as "the man I love" seemed more like a song cue than an introduction.

I was beginning to understand that all weekends would be difficult but nothing was like the sheer pandemonium of the Beethoven weekend. The music of Beethoven still draws the most ardent music lovers. That year Leonard Bernstein was conducting Beethoven's Ninth, which meant a legion of his fans would also come. Compounding the problem was the fact that parents' weekend at summer camp fell at the same time. There are about 150 camps in the Berkshire area, and thousands of parents make the trek from the cities to watch their children do the dead-man's float or execute a *pas jetée*.

Two days before the weekend, Steve received a call from an earnest young man who pleaded for a room, *anything.* "We're fully booked," Steve told him. "There's not even a mousehole within fifty miles," he added.

"I know. I've tried. How about your sofa?"

We were in the bedroom and Steve put his hand over the receiver. "This one will even take a sofa," he exclaimed. Then back into the telephone he said, "The only sofa we have is in the living room which is off the dining room and we don't close the restaurant until two A.M."

"That's okay," the young man insisted.

"I didn't mean I would rent it to you. I was only explaining.

107

There's no toilet. You'd have to wash up in the public men's room."

"Fine!"

"But you'd have to be up by eight when we start serving breakfast."

"Don't let anyone else use it," the young man replied. "I'll be there."

"Do you think he'll really show?" I asked.

"Never," Steve answered, and both of us promptly forgot it.

Friday afternoon, the day of the concert, Cornelia telephoned upstairs. She said, "Steve's not here and there is a young man who says he's booked the sofa in the living room." She must have cupped her hand around the receiver so that he couldn't hear because her voice almost faded out. "Do you think he might be from Riggs?" she whispered. Riggs was the local psychiatric clinic.

"Tell him I'll be right down," I told her.

His name was Gary. He was charming, attractive and had bright eyes and a little boy's grin. "Thought I wouldn't come?" he said.

"That's right," I replied. "But now that you're here, you can see that it would be impossible for you to sleep on the sofa."

Steve returned and we agreed to at least stow the young man's suitcase in our closet and to let him dress for the evening in our bathroom. After the concert he sat in the lounge listening to Steve until we closed. He was "into hi-fi," Gary told us. "Steve, you're great," he said, when the three of us were alone, "but the sound system is terrible."

"Someday, when we can afford it, we'll upgrade the equipment," Steve replied.

"But in the meantime you can't be heard to your best advantage," he insisted.

"You're right," I agreed, "and before next summer we should do something about it. But right now—where are you going to sleep?"

"Here." He grinned, flopping on the sofa.

It was impossible to turn him down. I went upstairs for linens and pillows, and we made up the couch together. It was a return to the days when Michael had brought his friends home from prep school for the weekend.

The next morning Gary was up when we came down for breakfast, his bed linens neatly folded. "How much do I owe you?" he asked.

"We can't possibly charge you for an uncomfortable night on a sofa. Forget it," Steve replied.

Gary started toward the door, and then turned back. "I'd like to put in a sound system for you. I could bring back my crew on Monday, if that's all right."

"We really can't afford it now," Steve replied quickly.

"We'll worry about that later," Gary said and then was gone.

"My God, what have I let myself in for!" Steve cried.

"He won't come back," I said.

Eight o'clock Monday morning Gary arrived with an engineer and an assistant in a station wagon crowded with speakers, amplifiers, microphones and wires. They worked through the day and most of the night putting together a sound box that would carry the music even upstairs. It was a complex system made up of the best components on the market. Steve paced our room nervously as they worked below. "I don't know what to say to this kid. I've told him over and over we can't afford what he's installing. Why, there are thousands of dollars of the finest equipment already installed, to say nothing of the labor."

"You can't ask them to pull it out now," I reasoned. "We'll have to pay them off gradually."

By early morning they had the speakers installed, the amplifiers and microphones connected, and were adjusting the system to Steve's voice. It sounded marvelous.

Around noon they packed up to leave. "Okay, Gary," Steve said, "now we have to talk about paying for all this."

"It's all taken care of," Gary replied and headed for the door.

"I can't let you pay for all that equipment. It's a fortune even if you get it wholesale: twelve speakers and a pre-amp, two mikes and God knows what else!" Steve followed him to the door.

"I own the company," Gary said, "and good sound and good music is my life. I like the way you sing and you should be heard properly. Okay? Oh, yeah, and you gave me a bed when I needed one most!"

"Nobody's ever done anything like that for me before," Steve managed.

Gary tapped Steve's shoulder in parting and winked at me. "Well, then I think it's about time someone did." He brushed by us and loped across the parking lot to the empty station wagon and his waiting staff.

Except for open rehearsals on Saturday mornings neither Steve nor I was ever able to hear a single Tanglewood concert, or to attend theatre at the Berkshire Playhouse or a ballet at Jacob's Pillow. When I went down to the kitchen for a cup of coffee, there was always some crisis that kept me there for an hour or more: the lunch chef hadn't shown and I had to prepare some food for the guests; the dishwasher wasn't working and I had to pitch in or there would be no dishes for lunch. If I sat by the pool, someone wanted a drink and the pool boy had disappeared. Passing through the lounge, on my way to our room, a guest would want to talk or there would be filled ashtrays and dirty dishes on the tables and no waitresses or chambermaids in sight. Refusing to come downstairs was no answer. Eventually I had to eat, and whoever brought a tray also came in with a list of complaints and requests from Rebecca, Yousef, the barman, Doug or a guest. My friends would exclaim about how marvelous it must be to live in an inn with round-the-clock service and no cooking. I would smile and say, "It has its advantages," but they were not easy to enumerate in the height of season.

110

Though daily life was difficult at the inn, the glory of the Berkshires in summer was fair compensation. The upstairs terrace, set in the high branches of the surrounding trees, overshot the view of the driveway and the main road and looked off to the distant rolling hills. We woke each morning to a beautiful tapestry of lush greens and violets and blues. When I felt I had to escape, I would take the dogs and disappear into our backwoods. The earth was springy there, the air musky. The woods were dense virgin timber, but there was a narrow path that bordered the brook and sunlight shafted through. The brook was clear, its banks thick with feathery moss. About a quarter of a mile in, the path opened onto a beautiful clearing. I would sit on a giant stump surrounded by delicate maidenhair and great sword ferns, listening to the forest sounds, the birds, the insects, the wind in the branches, the brook rushing over rocks.

In spite of Cathy's observation that running our house was like running an inn, Orpheus made many changes in my life. Some, I found, I could easily assimilate, but others I never got used to.

One difficult adjustment was that for every Lillian and Bernie there were ten guests who brought their personal problems to the inn and pulled Steve and myself in as mediators or advisers.

As we had only eight guest rooms, the houseguests would band together, and would be on a first-name basis with each other soon after arrival. Often a guest would answer the reservation phone or carry dishes into the kitchen. In this home-away-from-home atmosphere, we became not the innkeepers but the host and hostess. After one or two of our bone-dry martinis, they would tell us about their financial, marital, sex, children and parent problems. If you cared at all about people, you could not help becoming involved. Neither Steve nor I could change our own personalities, nor the fact that we cared.

There were those rare cases when we had nothing whatsoever in common with guests and, indeed, felt they would be happier elsewhere. We encountered our share of prejudice, for instance, and dealt with it directly. One couple objected strongly to our renting a room to a black man and his white wife. We asked the "objectors" to leave and they did. Another twosome did not "appreciate" rooming next to a homosexual couple. We also suggested they move on.

We found most trying those guests who were determined to change Orpheus to fit their own style. From the moment of her arrival, one woman shifted furniture and even talked Doug into letting her see what was in the basement, dragging back up to her room a curious assortment of furniture, lamps and china. She completely destroyed the country French image we had worked so hard to achieve.

Other visitors wanted to change our menu. The season had only begun when we received a call from a Mrs. Meltzer who said she would like a week's reservation and then proceeded to ask a million questions about the menu. She said that previously she and her friend, Mrs. Bromberg, stayed at Hillandale, an old resort near us that catered to senior citizens and served predominantly Jewish cuisine, but that Hillandale had no rooms available.

Steve explained that our cuisine was French, read her part of the menu and pointed out that we had no kitchen facilities to deal with special diets.

"Thank you, Mr. Citron," she said politely. "I'll discuss it with my friend, Mrs. Bromberg, and call you back."

Twenty minutes later she was on the telephone. "Mrs. Bromberg and I have decided to spend a week at your inn," she announced, "and are very much looking forward to meeting you."

The two women arrived in a mini-bus and alit from it wiping their brows with linen handkerchiefs. Their hair was freshly curled, their torsos tightly girdled. Mrs. Bromberg was small and sparrowy, Mrs. Meltzer tall and eaglelike. Steve met them at the door and took them onto the veranda while one of the staff carried their bags up to their room.

"Try one of our martinis," Steve suggested.

"Do you have ice cream sodas?" Mrs. Meltzer asked.

"No, but we serve coupe aux marrons." Steve smiled.

"What's that?" asked Mrs. Meltzer.

"Vanilla ice cream topped with brandied chestnuts."

"Maybe he has a little chocolate," Mrs. Bromberg bowed her head and whispered to her friend.

"I'm afraid not," Steve replied.

"Some caramel sauce then?" Mrs. Bromberg asked.

"I really think you'll like the coupe aux marrons," Steve insisted.

They were served two orders with the compliments of the house, and as each tasted the brandied chestnuts she made a face and carefully spooned the nuts off the ice cream and onto the saucer.

"Terrible," Mrs. Meltzer announced.

"I like chocolate," Mrs. Bromberg added.

I introduced myself and asked them if they would prefer iced coffee.

"We only drink Sanka," they replied.

"Darling, I think those ladies came here quite confident that no matter what was on the menu you would make special dishes for them," I said to Steve when we were alone.

"I told them that was impossible," he insisted. "You'll see, I'll convert them. They'll be speaking French and have a mania for escargots before they leave."

That night he sent them a split of champagne. They each took a polite sip. "Tell me," they asked Yousef, "do you have a little seltzer?"

Then they began ordering. "First," said Mrs. Meltzer, "we'll have some fruit cocktail."

"I'm sorry, but we don't have any on the menu," Yousef apologized.

113

"It says right here at the bottom"—she lifted the menu for him to see — "*fruit.*"

"Ah, yes," Yousef said carefully, "macédoine of fruit. That is for dessert."

"Is there a law against serving it first?" Mrs. Meltzer wanted to know.

"No, of course not," Yousef explained, "except that it is made with Triple Sec liqueur and might not start your dinner off well."

"Couldn't we have the fruit without the Triple Sec?" Mrs. Bromberg ventured.

"It's all prepared, I'm afraid," Yousef said.

"What fruits are in it?" Mrs. Meltzer inquired.

"Oranges, grapefruit, pineapple and strawberries," Yousef said.

"We'll take just the oranges and grapefruit—and maybe the cook can cut up a banana. I noticed you also have banana flambée on the menu, so you must have a few bananas. Then," Mrs. Meltzer rushed on, not giving Yousef a chance to object, "we want some onion soup, only make sure you put it through a strainer. Onions give us indigestion. And no cheese on it. Plain broth. And Mrs. Bromberg will have the chicken. Please tell the cook to broil it, no seasonings and no sauce. I'll have a chopped steak—"

"But, madame," Yousef finally interrupted, "we don't have chopped steak on the menu."

"You have filet and filet is steak, right?"

"Yes, but . . ."

"How difficult can it be to chop it? You have pâté. You must have a grinder," she reasoned, turning immediately away and beginning a conversation with Mrs. Bromberg.

Yousef found me in the gallery. "Steve tells me those ladies are booked for a week," he said, wiping his brow.

"Yes, that's right," I agreed.

114

"Tell me," he said, a gleam in his eye, "how do they feel about Arabs?"

After dinner they called me into the sitting room. "Miss Edwards," Mrs. Meltzer began, "we don't like to complain ..."

"Or start trouble," Mrs. Bromberg added.

"But it took such a long time to be served tonight. Maybe tomorrow we can order in the morning so the cook can have dinner ready at seven. It's nearly nine and we just got up from the table."

"Look, darling," Steve said to me later, "they're driving me up the wall. What shall we do?"

"I'll call around and see if I can find someplace else for them," I suggested.

Steve went back into the sitting room where the two ladies were playing casino, and sat down between them. "You know, Mrs. Meltzer," he began calmly, "you're going to have an uncomfortable week here."

"We know. We've already tested our beds and the mattresses are too hard," Mrs. Meltzer agreed.

"Well, maybe we could switch some mattresses," he said, trying to restrain his anger. "But I don't mean mattresses—I mean our menu. I don't think it is suited for your tastes, and with the rush before Tanglewood it is impossible to make anything special. I did tell you that on the telephone."

"We're not asking for *anything special,* just something simple," Mrs. Meltzer argued.

"It's not possible, Mrs. Meltzer. But don't worry, Miss Edwards has found you a wonderful accommodation in town, a place with plain American cooking. I'll return your deposit—call the dinner on me—and Doug will drive you over."

"You're a very stubborn young man," Mrs. Meltzer complained.

"And that's part of it," Steve countered. "I can't stand hostility. It puts me off my music."

115

"Who's hostile?" Mrs. Meltzer screamed. "All we want is a little broiled chicken."

"And some chocolate ice cream," Mrs. Bromberg added, nudging her.

"Jeannette is tired," Mrs. Meltzer continued, "and maybe we both are weary from the heat and the ride. That bus was so uncomfortable, and I had a fight with my son, Harold, before we left. He didn't want us to come here. But we like the place and you and we don't want to check out. After a night's rest, you'll see. It will all look better."

The next morning they were downstairs eating breakfast as we started out for our shopping tour. Mrs. Meltzer grabbed Steve by the arm. "Your housekeeper, Mrs. Gretchner, said you go into town to do the marketing every morning and Jeannette and me, we thought, if it wouldn't be an imposition, maybe we could ride along with you."

"We're already late," he grumbled.

Mrs. Bromberg pushed some zwieback (which was not on our menu) gallantly away from her. "We'll eat something a little later, Tiba," she said to Mrs. Meltzer.

They both rose from the table and followed Steve and me to the car. They sat huddled together in the back seat of the convertible, their handkerchiefs tied around their heads to keep their hair in place. Steve sped along the road to Pittsfield, glancing at them in the rear-view mirror as he stepped on the accelerator. Their hands flew to their heads to hold the handkerchiefs on, their bodies slunk down in the seat, but not once did they complain or ask him to put the top up or to slow the car down. When we dropped them in front of England Brothers, the only decent-sized department store in Pittsfield, he said, "I'll pick you ladies up in exactly two hours at this very spot." He added, "I have a lot of things to do as soon as I get back."

"Don't worry," Mrs. Meltzer announced, "we'll be Johnnies-on-the-spot. Jeannette, let's synchronize our watches."

116

They were waiting for us when we returned, waving their handkerchiefs, although they were visible from blocks away. Stacked around them were boxes and shopping bags in such profusion that I imagined them overwound and speeded up, running from department to department to get it all done within the two-hour time limit.

That night Steve set out two chocolate ice cream coupes, topping each with a healthy shot of crème de cacao. He brought it to their table himself. "I have created a sauce especially for you," he announced. The coupe quickly became their special dessert. On the third evening of their stay, by which time they were sampling most things on the menu, I heard Mrs. Bromberg ask Yousef, "Maybe you could tell the cook not to be so stingy with the sauce."

In the beginning they had spent their evenings in the sitting room playing casino, but now they would take the table nearest the piano and remain for at least two sets, "shushing" the noisy customers. Soon they knew many favorites in Steve's repertoire and would hum along to themselves, eyes dancing, hands tapping on the table. And every morning they drove into Pittsfield with us, sitting silently in the back and returning with more and more shopping bags filled with purchases. "My sister Birdie's daughter is having a tough time," Mrs. Bromberg would explain. "My son, Harold, has no taste on his own," Mrs. Meltzer would complain.

On the day that was to be their last at Orpheus, Mrs. Meltzer sat herself in the front seat beside Steve. I had no choice but to sit in the back with Mrs. Bromberg. Mrs. Meltzer had apparently elected herself spokeswoman. "Jeannette and I have been thinking about how we can say thank you. You've been so nice to us, driving us back and forth."

Mrs. Bromberg turned to me. "Perhaps he needs some pants shortened or buttons sewn on? I could do it when I get back to the inn," she offered.

"What we really want to say," Mrs. Meltzer said, "is that

we are planning to stay another week if you have room, and we want to be helpful."

"Well, I'll have to speak with our secretary to see if your room has been reserved or not," Steve hedged.

"Oh, we spoke to Miss Potts," Mrs. Meltzer nodded. "She said the room hadn't been reserved as far as she could see, and she would have to speak to *you* to make sure you hadn't rented it without informing her. But it sounds like you haven't, so I'll call Harold and tell him we won't be back for another week."

When they did depart they left behind various tokens of their affection: several boxes of zwieback, two egg cups, one plastic shower cap and a pair of men's golf shoes.

"Those can't belong to either Mrs. Meltzer or Mrs. Bromberg," I said accusingly to Mrs. Gretchner, who held up the shoes for me to see.

"I found them under one of their beds," she said with a sneer.

"They must belong to Mr. Davidson who had the room before them," I admonished.

"Did he write you to tell you they were missing?" she asked.

"No."

"Ummmm. Looks to me like a pair of the same kind of shoes I saw on Mr. O'Reilly who was in the next room to them ladies. I leave it to you, Miss Edwards, to figure out how they got under one of their beds," she said, and shuffled away before I could comment.

As the summer progressed we grew increasingly optimistic about our future. The inn was well booked and we were serving approximately 200 to 250 dinners on Saturday nights. Though Doug would complain bitterly about the abuse to the lawns, Steve and I loved to see the cars lined up on either side of the long driveway and cheered when there was no more room and the cars were forced to park on the highway.

We hired an all-night cleaner on weekends, but as the res-

118

taurant did not empty until after two, it never got a thorough cleaning. There was no time when all the dishes were clean or the soiled linen hampers empty, and there were always tons of garbage.

Somehow I got used to that but I never was able to accustom myself to the constant turnover of guests. You would just begin to learn that the Burtons were in Room 7 when suddenly they were gone and the room was occupied by the Leventhals.

At three or four in the morning Steve would tally the proceeds, turn off the lights and lock up. Unless Lex was with us, I would join him, sitting at the bar having a late snack, while he tried to balance the till in a manner that Paul would approve.

One night, when I had remained upstairs with Lex, Steve came loping up the stairs two at a time. He entered the room grinning broadly and turned the blue bank deposit bag upside down so that bills and change clattered and fluttered all over me on the bed.

"Guess how much we took in?" He beamed.

"I can't possibly guess. I didn't go downstairs tonight," I answered, blinking my eyes and straightening up.

"We took in thirty-three hundred and forty-six dollars and fifty-nine cents. I added it three times. I'll never forget it. It's the biggest night we've had, and you know what I've decided? Your birthday's next week and we can't properly celebrate with the inn open. But the day the inn closes, the day after Labor Day, we're flying to Europe. How's that?"

"Fantastic, darling, but can we afford it?"

"Look at this money," he said, taking a handful of bills and showering me with them again. "Haven't we worked like dogs? Don't we deserve a little special service ourselves? Let's go downstairs and break open a bottle of champagne!"

I slipped into a robe and the dogs pattered after us down the stairs and into the bar. The night cleaner looked up from his scrubbing with some surprise.

"Bring us a bottle of champagne from the cold room, Jim," Steve ordered, as though Jim was standing there in a tuxedo and we were guests.

"What does a bottle of champagne look like?" Jim inquired.

"Expensive," Steve replied. "Bring us the most expensive-looking bottle of anything in the cold room."

We drank an entire bottle of Dom Perignon and even gave the poodles a saucerful. An hour after we had crept tipsily upstairs, the breakfast chef called to ask if eggs were being delivered because there were only one dozen left. Ten minutes passed and Lex bounced in to get ready for day camp. By 8:00 A.M. Steve was off to the market for eggs and I was downstairs in the gallery, bleary-eyed as I totted up bills for the early morning checkouts.

During the next three weeks all either of us could think about was the trip to Europe. Cornelia had agreed to remain at Orpheus with her two girls while we were away. The inn would be closed but Mrs. Gretchner and a helper were to come in daily and give the place a thorough cleaning before we reopened for the foliage season. The dogs would be taken care of, and Cathy, who had come to live with us, planned to have a weekend party—so everyone was happy.

Early on the Friday morning before we were to leave, Steve and I drove into town to do the heavy shopping and to deposit the midweek receipts. In the bank, he walked over to me from the teller's window and shouted, "Hallelujah! We have an eighteen-thousand-dollar balance," not caring who heard him. He lifted me off my feet and twirled me around. "I am going to show you a Paris you've never seen," he promised.

But the season wasn't over. The rain began that morning and grew worse by late day, and with it came wind, thunder and lightning. By early evening the cancellations began to come in.

"So what," Steve shrugged. "One bad night in the entire season. You'll see. Tomorrow the sun will shine and Orpheus

120

will be jumping." I remembered his promise to win over Mrs. Bromberg and Mrs. Meltzer and decided that it was quite possible for him to make the sun shine.

Houseguests began checking out. It looked as though the Saturday night Tanglewood concert, the last of the season, might be canceled. Steve refused to be daunted.

Early Saturday afternoon the thick black coiled ropes of cloud disappeared and the sky turned a dull, leaden gray. The rains had stopped. Our remaining guests decided to don their bathing suits, take their martinis out to the pool and greet the sun, which they were certain would shine through momentarily.

We were in the kitchen when we heard the sound of thunder, distant, then closer. There was an ear-splitting crack that shook the house and a flash of lightning that seemed to come directly inside. The rain lashed down, and the guests trooped back from the pool just as the winds came roaring up the highway, blowing rain in angry gusts, snapping off branches of trees and tossing them across the driveway. Windows rattled and shutters creaked, but all of us inside soon became oblivious to the weather—perhaps aided by constantly refilled pitchers of martinis. The phone was out of order, and as it became quite clear that there would be no dinner business that night, we sent most of the staff home. Those who remained would spend the night in what empty rooms we had or on the couch in the sitting room.

At about eight o'clock the electricity went off and we ran around the inn lighting candles. The storm now seemed a grand adventure. No one appeared to notice the terrible nearness of each bolt of lightning, but one awesome crash brought us all up short. Doug and Steve, in black oilslickers, swinging a lantern before them, went out to investigate, looking like fishermen caught in a fierce storm.

Doug was distraught when they returned. The old oak tree at the foot of the driveway had been felled by the storm and lay straight across Route 7. Until the highway repairmen could remove it, no one could get through from either direction. There was nothing any of us could do, so Steve sat down at the piano and we all gathered round. Moments later the front door burst open, wind and rain sweeping through the downstairs.

"Is there a doctor in here?" shouted a young man who tore into the lounge.

Steve jumped up from the piano. "Is someone hurt?"

"My wife is in labor. We were on our way to the hospital, but the tree out front is blocking the road."

For some insane reason the voice of Butterfly McQueen in *Gone With the Wind* kept going through my head . . . "Not me, Miss Scarlett. I don't know nothin' about birthin' no baby!"

Four of us bundled up and struggled down to the road. The pregnant girl was no more than twenty and she was terrified. I got into the front seat beside her and tried to calm her, but it was impossible. A pair of headlights advanced from the opposite direction and a car came to a halt on the other side of the tree, facing us. It was the highway patrol who agreed to take the couple back to Great Barrington, where there was another hospital.

We wrapped the pregnant girl in whatever we could find— a lap blanket, her coat and a tarpaulin from the trunk of the car. With Steve, Doug, her husband and the highway patrol officers all in attendance, she was carried over the mammoth felled oak and placed safely in the back seat of the patrol car.

The next morning was glorious with sunshine, the air fresh and clear. A massive clean-up campaign was put into action and by early afternoon the driveway and pool were clean and the highway department had come along to cut up and remove the old oak. By evening, to our amazement, cars began to stream up the driveway.

Many of the staff had already left Stockbridge. We could never have made it through that night if our remaining houseguests hadn't helped. One tended bar, another answered the constantly ringing telephone and took reservations, while still another worked in the kitchen.

Monday was Labor Day and restaurant reservations came pouring in. By five that afternoon I could barely walk up the stairs. Storm damage had kept Mrs. Gretchner from coming in and I had made ten beds that morning. I had also washed stacks of pots and worked as "bar girl." Now the last house-guest had gone, Yousef was setting up the tables for dinner and Rebecca was getting a weary start in the kitchen. Steve insisted I sit down in the lounge, where he would bring me a drink.

"One drink and you'll have to carry me up the stairs," I moaned.

"Let's close," Steve said. "Tomorrow we leave for our holiday. We have to pack and we need some rest."

"But we have about twenty bookings for dinner," I protested.

"They'll just have to find someplace else to eat. I'm sending the staff home right now, pulling the blinds and putting a sign on the door."

"But, darling," I argued, "we also have a reputation. We can't just close with twenty reservations."

"Don't move," he ordered, heading for the basement. Ten minutes later he returned with a freshly painted sign. "There," he said, holding it for me to see. "No one can fault us after reading this sign":

Closed Because of a
Death in the Family

"That's terrible." I said. "And not true."

"Did you see Doug this afternoon when they were cutting up the old oak?" Steve bowed his head reverently. "It was as though a member of our Orpheus family had died."

We hung the sign in the entrance, locked all the doors,

turned off the downstairs lights, drew the upstairs blinds and packed by candlelight. A few people still came pounding on the door, but our ruse worked. The "intruders" withdrew.

We went down to the kitchen to fix ourselves a midnight dinner after our bags were packed, Biba and Krissy padding along at our heels. We prepared a feast of leftovers for them and scavenged the giant refrigerators for ourselves.

"We made it," Steve said as he munched a shrimp sandwich.

I started to cry.

He came to my side and put his arms around me. "Darling, what is it?"

"It will be beautiful here now. The sun will be shining and we can have the pool to ourselves. The woods will be cool and leafy and we're going to miss it all . . ."

"It's just two weeks," he soothed, "and we'll have the greatest holiday any two people could have." He beamed at me with such delight that my sadness passed and my thoughts turned to Paris and the new joys we were about to share.

PART

THREE

"**M**esdames et messieurs, nous allons atterrir à Orly en dix minutes," the voice of the captain filled the cabin. As he continued with landing instructions, I became apprehensive. I thought of Thomas Wolfe's admonition and wondered if I could "go home again," to Paris, my spiritual home. I would be showing the city to someone I loved, and as Gertrude Stein said: "Paris èst Paris est toujours Paris!" But what if my Paris had changed?

I found that in some outward ways it had—Les Halles was gone. There was a drugstore replacing my old Club de Paris. The Madeleine's grimy frieze had been scrubbed and unmasked for what it was—a second-rate copy of the Parthenon. Steel sculpture had been inappropriately set in the Tuileries. Mignon Lombard had retired to the South of France, taking Fernand with her.

But Paris was still the gay romantic, the sophisticate among cities—the witty, sad-beautiful charmer. Annè and I roamed her rues and environs. We ventured into the restaurant supply section and bought café filtre pots. We searched out antique stores and purchased Provençale copper bowls, and nineteenth-century brass bells. Everywhere we dined we made notes. We liked the intimacy of Nicolette et Raffetin, the elegant dessert cart in the entry at Taillevent, the cut of the waiters' coats at the Moniage Guilliume. We looked at it all with an eye to what could be taken back to Orpheus when we returned. I saw Paris

127

both as a man in love and as an innkeeper.

I discovered new things about myself. I was more confident, less restless and far happier than I had been in the Paris years of my youth. Taking stock of myself, I noted: I now shared a great love and was no longer alone in my life and my work. I had succeeded in communicating artistically with my students and my audiences. And I had money in the bank.

"Darling," I said to Anne, on our return flight, "isn't this too much happiness to last?"

"There you go with your Jewish guilt again." She smiled at me. "Of course, it's going to last." And she closed the subject and raised a toast to the future. She was still smiling when Cornelia met us at the door of the inn.

"The girls had such a good time." Cornelia grinned. "They slept in a different bed every night like Goldilocks. It's the first time either of them has had a room to herself, to say nothing of a swimming pool. They've had such fun that it will be hard for them to go home again."

"What about you?" I asked. "Did you enjoy it?"

"Oh, I swam, too. But what I enjoyed most was being able to straighten all the files and the books." Cornelia's eyes glistened with excitement and a broad smile swept over her face. "You can't imagine how many fall reservations and also how many bills came in at the close of the season. I made separate lists of each of your messages. And"—she took me by the hand and led me into the gallery "come see your desk. It's all in order, and just look at the ledger—everything is balanced beautifully."

It was as she said. Even the in and out baskets were empty. "Brava, Cornelia," I exclaimed. She beamed proudly. "Where are the bills you mentioned?" I asked.

"Oh, they're all filed," she replied.

"I don't know that that's such a good idea. Our restaurant bills are due ninety days after receipt and as Mrs. Gretchner would say—out of sight, out of mind."

128

"Oh, you don't have to worry about that. They're all paid."

"You paid all the bills?" I gasped.

"Yes. Every one. And you have—let me see," she reached into the bottom drawer of the desk for the check register and then put on her glasses. "You have a *two-hundred-and-thirteen-dollar-and-twenty-seven-cent balance.*"

"You paid over eighteen thousand dollars' worth of bills?" I repeated, in disbelief.

"Oh, I didn't pay them until I checked out every last item," she said seriously.

"You did what?" I shouted. Anne came running and stood staring at us. "Cornelia wrote over *eighteen thousand dollars'* worth of checks to cover all the bills," I screamed. "Bills that weren't due until late November. And on top of that I wrote checks in Europe. How will we ever get through the fall?"

Anne was taken aback but she still managed a soothing tone. "There's the foliage season coming. Cornelia said there were bookings. And at least there won't be any debts over your head."

"We're broke," I wailed. "What was that you said on the plane about Jewish guilt and happiness lasting?" I turned on Cornelia, shouting, "Why didn't you cable me?" My assault was interrupted by barking and yapping as the two poodles came bounding into the gallery.

"Stop yapping!" I shouted at them, at which point Biba squatted.

"Good Lord," Cornelia said, in thick New England nasal tones, "you terrified me—but you obviously scared the shit out of that poor little dog."

We stood there. Then Anne burst into laughter. It was only a moment before I realized how ridiculous the situation was and roared with her. Cornelia, at first tentatively and then wholeheartedly, joined in our hysteria.

"I iced a bottle of Moët," Cornelia said meekly. "It was supposed to be a welcome home." She quickly left the room.

"Hell"—I grinned—"I'm so used to being broke, I wouldn't know how to act with money in the bank anyway."

We managed to get through to foliage. In a way, Cornelia's action had been a blessing. When reservations dropped off we were grateful for the good credit we had established. Meanwhile, we had to think of some way to boost business.

"Why don't we turn the gallery into a movie theater and offer free films along with dinner?" I suggested.

"Remember that Chief Obie said we would need an extra exit if we showed films in that space. But we could use it as it was intended—as an art gallery. Why not have an art show with a gala opening and invite the local art critics and celebrities?" Anne suggested.

I liked the idea immediately and decided that we needed an artist who wasn't local so that the show would bring people from out of state to stay at the inn. The previous spring a commercial artist from Boston had been a guest. "Do you remember the etchings and drawings of Tom Mulligan?" I reminded Anne. "He was damned good and dying to break away from the commercial art he does for a living."

Neither of us could possibly have forgotten Tom— a brawny, articulate Irishman with a sharp wit, a strong tenor voice and a limitless capacity for whiskey. When we called him, he said he would be delighted to show at our gallery, and we set a date in mid-October.

We sent out announcements, and the reservations began pouring in: the Brian Mulligans, the Sean Mulligans, the Dennis Mulligans and so forth. I told Cornelia to be sure she listed first names on the reservation cards. Our guest book looked like the seating arrangements for an Irish wedding. Meanwhile I learned "Mother Machree" in anybody's key and ordered a case of Lochar's Dew.

There had been some previous bookings, one from a publisher and his wife who had read about us in *New York* magazine. They were to occupy the room next to ours. The minute they entered, carrying several suitcases and garment bags for their two-night stay and elbowing their way through a sea of convivial Mulligans in the bar, I knew we were in trouble. Mr. Publisher wore an English blazer and, somewhat bulldoglike, gripped a hand-carved pipe between his teeth, puffing away as he scrimmaged through the room. Mrs. Publisher had a complicated coiffure; her eyes were veiled in thick false lashes; and she was clothed in a form-fitting leather jumpsuit. Doug came running to help them bring the baggage to their room and I invited them for a welcoming drink. It was only five in the afternoon but the Mulligans were all drinking heavily and singing Irish ballads at the bar. I suggested that Anne and I and Mr. and Mrs. Publisher go into the living room so that we could get acquainted.

The conversation went something like this:

Mr. P.:   What a beautiful spot you have here. Reminds me a bit of the terrain of Devon.

Mrs. P.: Oh, Artie, look, they have the local paper. (Picking up the *Berkshire Eagle*) Let's see what sales they're having. (To Anne) What kind of a store is England's?

Mr. P.:   (Before Anne could reply) How far are we from Williamstown? I hear there's a fine collection of Renoirs at the Clark Museum.

Mrs. P.: (Before I can answer) There's a Robert Redford film in Pittsfield, Artie!

Me: You're a publisher, I understand. Anne is an author, you know?"

Mrs. P.: (To Anne) Do we dress for dinner? I spoke to your secretary from New York and she said anything was suitable, which confused me even more! I brought several kinds of dresses—just in case. Would a long dress be most appropriate?

131

Mr. P.: (Standing) Is there a private phone I can use? I'll charge it to my credit card.

They both left then, he for the phone in the office, she, presumably, to make preparations for dinner.

We had invited the press and widely advertised the opening. By six-thirty the gallery was jammed, the innumerable Mulligans adding to the congestion.

Mr. and Mrs. Publisher entered. All eyes turned from the Mulligan etchings to Mrs. Publisher—dazzling in a mirrored sheath so tight that she looked like a mermaid just risen from the sea.

"Is there another private telephone?" Mr. Publisher asked me, looking rather disturbed.

"In our room. You're welcome to use it," I offered. He immediately left Mrs. P. standing alone in the center of the room.

Gradually the crowd in the gallery moved to the bar and lounge for drinks and dinner. Mrs. P. stood smiling nervously, a glass of champagne in her hand. Mr. P. had not returned. Anne went over and spoke to her. I was called into the kitchen and when I returned Mrs. P. was gone.

"She went into the bar with one of the Mulligans." Anne looked strangely concerned.

"Anything wrong?" I asked.

"I'm not sure," she said enigmatically, and kissed me in front of the remaining art viewers. "I love you," she whispered, "and am feeling very smug that we're so together."

When I went into the bar Mrs. P. was moving from man to man in a quest for attention. One could feel the icy stares of the Mulligan women. Mrs. P. finally edged her way in between Tom and Maureen Mulligan, murmuring something about how good Tom's etchings were.

Tom's youngest brother was Father Liam Mulligan, an attractive, quiet man who for this weekend was wearing "civilian

132

clothes." He had just entered the bar, and to avoid what looked like a brewing battle between Maureen and Tom, I steered Mrs. P. toward him. "This is Tom's brother, Liam," I said, and left them.

A short time later they were seated at one of the banquettes with a disgruntled Tom and Maureen. It was impossible not to notice that Mrs. P.—seated between the two men—was playing the vamp. She pressed close to Liam and then turned and stared up adoringly at Tom. Mr. P. entered the lounge and caught his wife's amorous display. I was expecting a confrontation and stepped forward to deflect him, but Mr. P. sauntered past his wife's table without even glancing her way and went directly into the bar.

About fifteen minutes later I sat down at the piano for my first set. The banquette was directly in my line of vision. I froze in horror. Mrs. P. was standing in front of the table, Father Liam beside her in a position that indicated he had risen to let her pass. Suddenly, with a coquettish laugh and a bold gesture, she swept her hand downward, unzipped his fly, reached forward and pulled his penis out. Each of these movements was reflected in the small mirrors of her dress.

Liam turned a deep vermilion and quickly lowered his hands, looking for the moment like a camp version of "September Morn," and ran from the room. When he had not returned a half-hour later, two of his brothers went out to fetch him. He was brought back pale and shaken, and was seated in the center of an impregnable Mulligan circle.

Mrs. P. went into the bar. "Artie," she said to her husband, "come sit with me in the lounge." He didn't even turn around. Sitting at the vacant end barstool she drank steadily, trying her charms on whomever she could. She was still seated there when Mr. P. left the bar.

About a half-hour later, Anne came into the gallery where I was talking to Tom Mulligan about the drawings we had sold that night.

"What's that hammering?" I asked, alarmed.

"Mr. P.'s locked his wife out of the room and she's determined to get in," Anne reported. "It's terrible. I can't stand it. It makes me want to cry."

Finally the pounding stopped and I sent Anne to bed while I closed up. But as I turned out the outside lights I was conscious of a shimmering silhouette in the half-dark. Mrs. P. stood there—a pathetic mess, her hairdo collapsed, her mascara settled into clown spots beneath her eyes. "They all hate me," she said, her voice on the edge of tears.

"Who hates you?" I asked.

"All the guests. Artie locked me out and I went to all their rooms and asked them to let me sleep on the floor, *anywhere*. They all refused."

I was furious with her. How dare she impose on my guests! But then, standing there, looking at that sad creature in her mirrored gown, I felt sorry for her, for all the people in the world who were not in communion with each other. I went upstairs, brought some linens and made up the sofa as a bed.

Liam did not come down for breakfast, but all the other Mulligans did. Mrs. P. ate alone, still dressed in her mirrored sheath. It broke my heart to look at her there, sitting silently, dipping her croissant into her coffee. The early-morning Berkshire sunlight pouring in made her dress sparkle and gleam, and it also accentuated her dried make-up, her lined and smudged face, her eyes brimming with tears. Then she rose wearily and in almost a catatonic state started for the doorway.

"Are you all right?" I asked.

"I think I'll wait for Artie in the car," she said, her voice choked. "I don't know if he'll drive me home."

Artie came down in about an hour, looking relaxed. I told him his wife was in the car, but he made no rush to join her. Finally, after he had paid the bill and tipped everyone lavishly, he took me aside. "I'm sorry," he said simply. "Maybe, if you'll allow us, we could come here again under different circumstances. I had hoped that getting away to an inn like this might turn the tide." He grinned nervously. "Maybe next time, eh?"

After their autumn brilliance, the leaves turned a jaundiced yellow, withered, dried and fell within days. November is the worst month in the Berkshires, a bleak, threatening gray limbo between the lovely fall display and the beauty of the New England winter. The only bright spot seemed to be the approach of Thanksgiving.

"What are we going to do about the holiday?" Anne asked.

"We'll advertise a French Thanksgiving," I beamed with inspiration.

"A French Thanksgiving?" She laughed.

"What is Thanksgiving? A banquet, right?"

She looked dubious.

"The idea is to gorge yourself on Thanksgiving. That's a banquet, a celebration. And if Americans accept the Statue of Liberty, a French gift to us, why not a French Thanksgiving?"

I took her by the elbow and sat her down at the table. "Let's plan a really sumptuous meal. We'll spare nothing. And we can send off a menu to all the guests who've ever registered here. They can reserve a table for the entire evening, come at any hour and eat until they burst. We'll serve champagne and wine and after-dinner liqueur. And while we're at it we can do the same thing for Christmas and New Year's Eve. "How about that?" I asked, excited.

"I think it might work. In fact, I like it!" Anne agreed.

With that, she got up and brought us coffee and a pile of cookbooks. We scoured every one, getting ideas, constructing our menus. I insisted that the *pièce de résistance* be goose.

"Have you ever cooked a goose?" Anne wanted to know.

"How difficult can it be?" I dodged.

"I never made one but I had it from time to time in England," she said in a skeptical voice. "Most often it was greasy, tough and really did not serve many people."

135

"Ours will be smashing," I insisted. But I bowed to Anne's wishes and planned also to serve turkey for Thanksgiving.

We created three separate menus for the three holidays, each of which was two typewritten pages long. We entitled the Thanksgiving menu

ORPHEUS ASCENDING

PRESENTS

A FRENCH TRIBUTE TO

AMERICA'S THANKSGIVING

and included tons of courses. We used gold paper for Thanksgiving, green for Christmas and blue for year's end. Several hundred copies of each were xeroxed and sent out with an accompanying "letter of invitation," an RSVP and a deposit request. The response was heavy for Christmas and New Year's Eve, but not for Thanksgiving.

"Maybe we were wrong about Thanksgiving," Anne ventured. "Maybe most Americans want a traditional holiday meal."

"We included turkey," I chided.

"Yes, but there's no cranberry sauce or pumpkin pie."

"They'll come," I said. "They just don't want to make reservations in advance. It will be a last-minute crowd."

By Thanksgiving week we had only a meager number of bookings, but I refused to believe that anyone could resist overindulging themselves on Thanksgiving with the great gourmet delights we had on our yard-long menu.

We began cooking on Monday and continued right through Thursday morning. There were just the two of us in the kitchen, working side by side for twelve hours each day. We baked rolls and bread and our own gâteaux, prepared dozens of hors d'oeuvre, blended béchamels and thick Mornays, strained and stirred the fresh pumpkin soup, beat the cream and egg whites for the Chantilly and meringue toppings, peeled the fresh vegetables and pitted the fruits. Cathy came home from school with her lively Labrador retriever, and the three dogs followed her around as she decorated the mantels with harvest fruits and strung streamers of dried leaves and flowers above the windows. We placed candy dishes everywhere, arranged cut flowers and filled crystal glasses with cigarettes. The banquet table stretched the full length of the lounge. In the entrance our largest silver platter was heaped with fresh and dried fruits and nuts. A bar with complimentary champagne, apéritifs and after-dinner liqueurs was set up in the gallery.

By 10:00 A.M. on Thanksgiving Day we had only eight dinner and one room reservations. I was stuffing one of the three geese with oysters and Anne was preparing one of the four twenty-six-pound turkeys for roasting when I noticed the snow. "What could be more perfect?" I crowed. "The grounds will look like they're straight out of Currier and Ives. And what could be more irresistible to city people than dining cozily in an old country inn while looking out at a slight covering of dusty snow on the ground?"

"Dinner in front of their own fireplace, central heating and no need to drive on slippery roads," my darling replied.

Rebecca arrived about noon to help us. "Wow!" she said as she beat her hands against her body to bring back the blood. "There's going to be a blizzard. I almost didn't make it! The wind is terrific and you can't see a foot in front of the windshield!"

The telephone rang. It was Johanna Weiss. She had postponed her call, hoping the weather would break. "It's terrible in New Jersey," she said. "We won't be driving up." That meant we had no room guests. By one in the afternoon the aroma of roasting turkey filled the inn. The inside of all the windows were coated with steam from the warmth of the kitchen and the blazing fireplace. Almost every reservation had called in to cancel. The storm grew worse. Yet Yousef arrived, followed by his assistant, the bartender, the kitchen help and the busboy. New Englanders never let a blizzard interfere with their duties. I was optimistic that it was also a sign that the local people would come by. "How many tables shall I set up, Steve?" Yousef asked, motioning glumly at the windows.

"Set them all," I replied stoutly.

I went back into the kitchen and sat down dejectedly. Anne was putting the finishing touches on a gâteau Chantilly. There she sat, hair gathered up and secured with a chopstick, fingers coated with whipped cream. Lex was standing beside her, tossing chocolate jimmies on the cake. Cathy was decorating an hors d'oeuvre platter. Rebecca sang as she chopped onions for a quiche, and the radio blasted rock music. I thought of Thanksgiving at home in Trenton, the big table with the children and grandchildren all around, the warmth and the love. Here we had cooked for a week, and in spite of my bravado it looked as if none of the people we had cooked for were going to make it. I glanced over the counter at Anne.

"Maybe I was foolhardy," I said. But then I thought, "Lex is here and Cathy—Anne's by my side—the staff was loyal—and it *is* Thanksgiving."

"Of course!" I shouted out loud.

"Hey, Doug!" I called. Doug appeared from the back kitchen, where he was trying to fix the leaking ice machine. "Take down the OPEN sign and turn off the spots. Why should we sit around waiting for customers when it's Thanksgiving?" Doug immediately disappeared to carry out my order. "And Cathy, get on the phone and invite all the staff who aren't here to come with their families. Tell them to put their own turkeys in their freezers. Call Mrs. Gretchner and Cornelia." Cathy let out a cheer and dashed out of the kitchen. "Rebecca, use the second line and call your boyfriend and then have Yousef call his family." Rebecca whooped as she hurried to the telephone.

Cathy poked her head back in. "Mrs. Gretchner wants to know if she can bring Ronald?"

"Who's Ronald?" I asked.

"She says he's her fiancé," Cathy replied.

"Hey, Leticia has been holding out on us!" I laughed. "Sure, tell her to bring Ronald."

Anne and I were alone in the kitchen. "I think I love you more this minute than ever before." She grinned.

"It's going to be a fantastic Thanksgiving," I promised.

"It already is."

Two hours later our entire inn family was seated in the lounge. Lex was on my left, and next to him Cathy, acting like his big sister and helping to cut his food. Yousef and his brood were on the far end. Mrs. Gretchner and her fat, pink Ronald sat in the middle. Anne and I excused ourselves frequently to get up and serve. When Yousef passed the turkey, one of Cornelia's girls asked for the cranberry sauce, and before Cornelia could give a withering look to her daughter, I recognized our folly. Of course. There *had* to be cranberry sauce on Thanksgiving! And there should have been sweet potatoes and pumpkin pie. Soupe à l'Amérique simply did not make it, even if it was made of fresh pumpkins and cream. I went to the pantry myself and brought back a can of cranberry sauce.

Never did so few people eat so much or so lavishly. We had cooked for over a hundred and we were only twenty-nine. The dinner was fantastic. Except for the geese. Anne and I had each taken a small piece, and so had Yousef. Anne's worst fears were realized. It was greasy, tough and terribly scrawny. Cathy, with my permission, went into the kitchen with the geese, deboned them and set them down so the dogs could have their own Thanksgiving.

Although the snow continued, nobody felt like going home. By midnight we had become a convivial group, indeed. The kids sprawled asleep on various chairs and the adults had a

139

sing-along. Finally, when we could see the storm was not going to abate, everyone chose the room he or she wanted for the night.

One afternoon in mid-December, Mrs. Gretchner cornered me. "I don't know how to say this"—she reddened—"but Ronald feels we should get married right away."

"He seemed like a nice man," I said. "But what's the hurry?"

"I figure at my age you don't get opportunities too often. I'd better strike while his iron is hot."

I kept a straight face. "Are you trying to tell me you'll be leaving, Leticia?"

"Well, yes. But I could stay through the winter if you really need me. Actually, since Mrs. Edwards and then Miss Potts joined you it's almost like four's a crowd. Ronald wants us to retire to Florida and it might do me good to sop up that sunshine."

"That sounds fantastic, Leticia. But listen," I said a bit hesitantly, "do you think you and Ronald know each other well enough? I mean . . ."

"Have we spent the night together? Now, Mr. Citron, would you think I'd buy a pig in a poke?"

Though we had been a commercial failure for Thanksgiving, things looked promising for Christmas and New Year's Eve. Obviously our former guests did not have the same feeling about these two holidays as they did about Thanksgiving because the response was extremely good. The inn was solidly booked for both holidays, and dinner reservations for the banquets were coming in heavily. A friend of ours owned a nearby inn which he closed for the winter. After discussing it with Anne, I talked to him about renting it to us for the holidays to give us more rooms. Guests lodging there would pay lower rates, but they would have their meals with us, the use of the bar and, of course, the holiday banquet. We soon filled all the additional rooms.

This time Anne and I would really have a hundred people to cook for, and the Christmas menu was both exciting and complicated.

141

La Quiche Flamande
green squash and onions
baked in a
Belgian country pie

Les Pommes de Terre Jaunes
sweet potatoes baked with
cranberries, oranges and
Cointreau

Les Haricots Verts
aux Noix
buttered fresh
string beans with
hazelnuts and walnuts

Les Choux Suédoise
fresh steamed red cabbage
in a sweet-sour sauce
with tiny meatballs

La Salade à Gogo
a salad buffet of mixed greens, beets,
greenbeans and onions, cucumbers and dill,
carrots and paprika eggs served with
Roquefort and our own Orpheus dressing

Les Entremets
Greek and Italian olives, pickles, peppers

Les Pains
Home-baked rolls
and crusty French bread

La Confiture
French honey
and quince preserves

La Bûche de Noël
traditional French
pinwheel cake
frosted in mocha cream
and shaped like a yule log

La Tarte d'Orphée
our own creation:
chocolate cheesecake
with whipped cream
and Tia Maria

La Mousse au Citron
fresh lemon mousse with whipped cream

Le Plateau
de Fruits Suprême
a platter of fresh fruits,
nuts and dried
and candied fruits

Fromage
assorted imported cheeses
and crackers

Café   *Thé*   *Café Filtre*

142

Champagne and Burgundy
Will Be Served Throughout Dinner at
No Additional Cost to
Our Guests

Prix Fixe
$23.00 per person,
including cocktail, champagne, burgundy,
as many helpings from our table as you desire,
and all taxes and gratuities
Continuous service, Christmas, December 25,
from 4:00 P.M. to 9:00 P.M.

We strung our two biggest pine trees with red, white and blue lights, and cut one of our own firs from the backwoods—placing it in the breakfast room where it scraped the ceiling, and then decorating it with beautiful handmade ornaments and spun sugar candies purchased from Cornelia's girls. I had been lulled into expecting much of the same family ambiance that Thanksgiving had created, but Christmas that year was an entirely different matter.

Guests filled the public rooms from early morning to late night. Gifts began to flow out from the base of the tree like a river flooding from its banks as the guests placed their own gifts beneath it. There was hardly room for family gifts. On Christmas Eve, when we liked to open our packages, there were so many people surrounding the tree that Anne, Lex, Cathy and I (Anne's son, Michael, was coming up for New Year's weekend) carted all our presents up to our room and opened them on the bed. The next day Orpheus was so packed and the banquet had such a turnout that neither Anne nor I got to sit down with the kids. We didn't eat until after the last guest was gone, the kids were asleep and we had returned to the kitchen to prepare for the huge breakfast crowd we had to serve in less than eight hours.

"Well, this time the banquet was a success," Anne said as

we turned out the lights together. "Are you happy?"

I paused and placed my hands on her shoulders. "Are you?" I asked.

"Happier than I have ever been," she replied, "but I still hated eating our holiday dinner in the kitchen."

I was envious of all the other families in Stockbridge—hell! in the world—who had opened their packages under the Christmas tree, who had been able to watch their sons play with their new toys on Christmas morning and who had sat surrounded by their loved ones at Christmas dinner. But I was unable to admit it, even to Anne. We went silently up to our room and set the alarm for early the next morning when we would have approximately fifty people for breakfast and all those checkouts to handle by lunch. As I climbed exhaustedly into bed, I mused that at least Paul, the accountant, would approve.

There was less than a week for us to get Orpheus, ourselves and the menu into shape for New Year's. Once again we had taken over the other inn and had filled it. New Year's Eve had the feeling of the big Tanglewood Beethoven night. We were jammed and desperately understaffed. Michael pitched in at the bar, Cathy helped in the kitchen, and Anne and I never sat down for a minute. The one amusing incident in the evening was Cornelia's entrance (I had asked her to be my guest at dinner). She came in looking like a femme fatale—hair loose, eyes lined with iridescent make-up, a boa draped around her bare shoulders, and high-heeled shoes that made her walk as though she was tipped forward. She sat down dramatically at the bar.

"A triple martini," she ordered, winking at our bartender.

Suddenly he recognized her. "Cornelia!" he called out, and then promptly went into spasms of laughter. Cornelia took no offense and after two triple martinis was acting the role she had created for herself.

Our New Year's Eve menu included a massive buffet at 9:00

144

P.M., a five-course meal at 1:00 A.M. and a breakfast of onion soup, French bread and champagne at 4:00 A.M. At about a quarter to four I took Yousef aside. "You better tell the kitchen to start heating the onion soup," I advised him.

"Steve," Yousef replied, "there is only one way to get your guests to absorb anything more."

"What's that?" I asked.

"Lay them down on the floor and pour it over them."

Still, in spite of Yousef's disbelief, much of the onion soup was consumed, and there were those who remained until morning to partake of our elaborate New Year's Day breakfast buffet.

The year-end holidays had been a business success and yet they left me with a gnawing discontent. The thrill of spreading the word of Orpheus was no longer there for me. Still, it was good to be in the black for a change, and I called Paul to tell him the good news.

"Orpheus is in the black! Hooray!" I said.

"From your mouth to God's ear!" he answered.

Somehow the message did not get through, because by early January the country was in the throes of a serious gas shortage, car travel was limited and there was the possibility that gas would be rationed. Some inns advertised gas with their package deals, but we were in no position to do that. Whatever reservations we already had were canceled by travelers who were afraid they would be stranded in the snowy Berkshires. And no new reservations came in.

During the second week of the gas shortage Anne and I decided it would be best to close the inn until the situation eased. But although the inn was not open for business, insurance premiums continued, mortgage payments had to be met, fuel paid for and at least a small staff maintained. It didn't take very long for our bottom line to return to its habitual crimson.

PART

FOUR

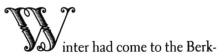inter had come to the Berk-
shires. I loved the fresh snowfalls and the flinty gray sky, the
smell of dry wood burning in the fireplaces and the trails of
chimney smoke that feathered the roof like the fine plumes on
a Victorian lady's hat.

But heating a huge place like Orpheus in the winter, even
though we were closed, was an expensive luxury we could not
afford. We turned off the heat at night and kept it at a minimum during the day. With chill winds sweeping under the
windows and doors, whipping my bathrobe around my trembling legs, I would chatter my way downstairs and into the
kitchen in the mornings to make a strong, hot pot of coffee
while Steve laid fires in the three hearths.

I had always harbored the idea that I was a most self-suffi-
cient woman and that my involvement in my writing was such
that I would never feel lonely. But every Monday through
Wednesday when Steve was in New York I felt overwhelmed
by loneliness. Cornelia came in every day, and there was
Nancy, a lovely young local girl who had assisted Mrs.
Gretchner and now had replaced her. In the evenings Steffi
often visited, or if Norman was on a lecture tour, Carol and I
would dine together. But without Steve, Madison Square Garden during a Barnum and Bailey circus performance would
have seemed a lonely, forlorn place. Also, an empty country inn
after the crowds of summer was disconcerting, and being alone

in it—winterbound and isolated—was at times frightening.

One night I was curled up in bed editing some work when I heard sounds in the attic rooms. The dogs roused themselves, and growling and barking, slunk to the locked bedroom door and howled. The wind rattled the shutters and rapped at the windows. "It's only the wind," I said aloud. "Come back." Ignoring my command, Biba began to dig furiously at the crack between the door and the rug, trying to burrow her way out.

I tied my bathrobe belt tighter around me, and grabbing the fire poker, slowly creaked the door open and peered down the long, dark hallway. I turned on the hall light and stood trembling. The sounds came from upstairs again, this time ghostlike. "Ooooooooooo—Ooooooooooo!" Both dogs scooted past me to the closed door at the foot of the third-floor stairway, and began to claw at it. I don't know what madness possessed me but I followed them down the corridor, clutching the poker.

"Who's there?" I called loudly.

"Ooooooooooo—Ooooooooooo!"

Biba threw herself against the door. Krissy sat back on her haunches and howled.

"It's only the wind," I repeated.

Terrified, yet with a feeling of self-possession, I opened the door. Two eyes glared up at me from the darkness. I could not make out what the creature was, but I was immediately thankful it had not sprung to attack me. Biba and Krissy danced behind me, barking, circling, pawing at the hem of my robe.

The thing fluttered wings, and I dropped the poker in terror, whereupon it rose in the air and flew over my head and into the hallway.

It was an owl, now perched on the hallway chandelier, glaring menacingly down at us.

I swept the dogs under my arms, ran to my room and bolted the door. Then I slid the television set in front of it and turned the sound as high as it would go.

The owl was gone the next morning. Cornelia, who was not

afraid of any country creature, went over the house from bow to stern before I would come out of the bedroom.

February 10 was Steve's fiftieth birthday. I decided, since the inn was closed, we should invite many of our out-of-town friends for the weekend. I planned a huge party for Saturday night. The menu was Chinese and, therefore, unlike anything we normally served at Orpheus. It meant ordering Oriental ingredients from New York, but when you like to cook there is a marvelous excitement in preparing dishes that are not on the menu every night.

Lex had a great time helping me make the hundreds of wontons and spring rolls I was serving along with the lobster rumaki and Chinese spareribs. There was also to be stir-fried shrimp with lobster sauce, lion's head (which are large pork balls), Szechuan chicken, steamed bass with fermented black beans, fried rice and Chinese vegetables.

I wanted the traditional birthday cake but Cathy recalled a Chinese bakery not far from her school that made a fabulous rice cake. I ordered one large enough to serve fifty people, which the bakery insisted they could bake. Cathy was to pick the cake up on her way home from Vermont for the festivities.

The party preparations made me realize the joys of a restaurant kitchen. There was plenty of space in the refrigerators and room in the freezer; enough burners and ovens to cook everything at once; heating trays and serving platters galore; numerous large pots and long-handled utensils; scads of counter space and—most wondrous of all—a professional dish-washing machine that did the dishes in ninety seconds.

Remembering his opening night at Orpheus, Steve encouraged the guests to work behind the bar for half-hour shifts. Everyone clamored to get his or her name on the time schedule.

I can't recall giving or attending a more successful party. Cathy, however, looked concerned when she came in with the cake. And when Steve started to cut it, the knife stuck halfway through. The Chinese bakery had quadrupled the ingredients without realizing this can often ruin the chemical balance of the recipe. The rice birthday cake was a disaster. We ended up freezing it and feeding bits of it to the birds. It lasted all winter.

Never had the Berkshires known a colder winter. The wind continued to seep under doors, through closed windows and beneath loose floorboards. The dogs refused to go more than a few feet from the front door and slept so close to the fireplace that I was always frightened they would wake up with roasted tails. In spite of the fact that President Nixon announced it was patriotic to shiver through those bitter months in support of national conservation, I was not about to freeze to death. We sealed off most areas but kept our room and the downstairs above the decreed sixty-eight degrees during the day. The price of fuel then doubled.

We ordered more wood, planning to lower the heat and keep the hearths going all day. The price of firewood immediately tripled. We each wore several sweaters and two pairs of socks, and Cornelia knitted jackets for the dogs.

Before the next winter we would have to insulate the inn, but meanwhile there was always the fear of the pipes freezing and bursting. One night, in spite of all our efforts, they did. Thereafter one sink in the kitchen spouted only cold water and the other only hot, and as the two sinks were separated by the entire room, kitchen work was not easy.

The plumber who had installed the "modern" heating and plumbing in the inn some thirty-five years before became our most constant visitor, for besides our frozen pipes and leaking radiators the great old black furnace in the basement was suffering grievously.

Neither of us was the slightest bit mechanical and we attempted to overcome this by memorizing every word of instruction that Joe, the plumber, had to impart. We tended that huge grizzly bear of a heater as if our lives depended on it. And, in truth, they did. The furnace was gasping its last breath and to replace it would mean an expense of well over $3,000. With the inn closed, and our balance sheet in its usual state, there was no way we could afford such an expense before another season. We could only hope to nurse that heater through the winter and spring. "The main thing," Joe had warned us, "is *never* to let the water in the gauge go below that red mark."

We were standing in front of the sweating black giant, its big pipes groaning. "You see," Joe explained, as simply as he could, "inside this burner is a ball of fire, and around it is a casing of water. The water"—he gently rapped a pipe— "comes from here. This valve controls its flow. If you let the water go below the red mark *there*"—he pointed to a glass gauge that looked like a thermometer—"there won't be water to cool off the ball of fire and the boiler could easily crack from the intense heat." He had his hat in his hand and shook his head. "Mighty beautiful piece of machinery, but looks like its time has almost come."

We had to check the gauge every few hours. Joe had patched up the leaks in the heater but more would appear all the time, quickly lowering the water beneath the red mark. At night we just had to pray. Steve would go down to the basement and feed it water before we went to bed, and I would wrap myself in several layers of clothing and sleepily tend it first thing in the morning. There were many mornings when I was on the telephone calling Joe before seven. He would come running with his bag of tools, his shirttails flying, his lumber jacket open, a red wool hat pulled down over his ears. In his size-twelve boots (Joe was almost as large as the heater!), he would scurry back and forth to his truck for additional "surgical equipment."

"It went below the red mark," I would shout above its rattlings and groanings.

"One of you will simply have to set an alarm and give it a middle-of-the-night feeding," he warned.

*   *   *

There is a different sound to spring rain in the Berkshires. It is a great, soft sigh that spreads from the foot of the hills, feathery and gentle, not whipping the trees and lashing the shutters and clapboards as the winter rain had. The snow melted; frogs croaked in the swimming pool; an owl, perhaps my midnight intruder, hooted without menace; and a warm sun glistened in the morning on the moist emerald tips of the fir trees and the white trunks of the birches.

I was happy and contented. We had at least nursed the furnace through the winter. Doug touched up the paint on the winter-worn clapboards and mended the leaks in the roof. The gas shortage seemed to have abated and we decided to reopen. We did so, however, with a small measure of reluctance.

During the few months the inn had been closed I had unpacked some of my favorite treasures and placed them in the downstairs rooms. And one crazy night when Steve and I were both tending the furnace in the basement he had taken me into the wine cellar, and from under some shelves dragged out boxes that contained art objects collected on a Far East tour when he had traveled one year as an American jazz expert for the United States Information Agency. At 1:00 A.M. we had carried up a Siamese shiva, a marble Buddha, Vietnamese pitchers, Indian rubbings and Venetian vases and distributed them throughout the house alongside my French and English antiques. Now they all had to be packed away and stored.

Also, Cathy had spent her spring vacation with us and I had loved the feeling of walking by the room she had chosen and seeing it alive and familiar with her clutter. When the inn reopened, that room had to be emptied, the contents stored, the atmosphere transformed to anonymity.

It had been a year since I had moved into the inn, and during that time there had been many guests I would not have invited into my own home because they were boring, bigoted or boorish. Once you pay your fee for an innkeeper's license, however, you leave yourself open to such abuse. An innkeeper does not have the right to ask for references.

Early that season Cornelia took a telephone reservation from someone who said her name was Rosamond Roosevelt. She had elaborated: "I am a niece of Eleanor and Franklin." It sounded pushy, but if a guest said she was Rosamond Roosevelt we did not ask for her driver's license or passport. And if she claimed first-family connections we did not require a genealogical chart.

She walked—or rather, *trailed*—up the driveway, carrying only a carpetbag. Her hair was loose and flying, and she was dressed in a long, billowy white dress that looked like a night-gown and that flapped about her booted feet.

"If you had called from town," I said as I greeted her, "we would have been happy to send someone to fetch you."

"Oh, I never accept rides in strange cars," she replied, wide-eyed.

I took Steve aside and confided that the young woman—she was in her early twenties—disturbed me. "She has a strange air of distraction," I said.

"I noticed that, too," he admitted, "but we can't ask her to leave without a better reason than that."

While we had been closed Rebecca had taken another job, and we had hired a young, inexperienced cook named Johnny. A track star at school and well over six feet tall, he made up in dexterity and speed what he lacked in cooking knowledge. Johnny worked without a kitchen assistant, and as he loped into the larder, stirring pots on the way, depositing food in the freezer, managing to return with an apron filled with onions, pâté loaves balanced in his one free hand, he looked somewhat like a juggler. He could chop ten pounds of onions in nothing flat while watching food in two ovens, the broiler and on all the burners. Sporting a winning smile and possessing a contagious laugh and a great sense of humor, he had sex appeal that rose above the scent of garlic and raw onions. All the ladies loved

155

Johnny—and Rosamond Roosevelt was no exception.

Although we had a sign outside the kitchen door that read STAFF ONLY, it was generally ignored by Orpheus guests, who went into the kitchen on a variety of excuses—fear of immediate malnutrition, dehydration or smiting blows by their mother's ghost for not returning their dirty dishes to the kitchen. But in all truth, they simply could not overcome their curiosity to see a restaurant kitchen.

Lunch had already been served when Rosamond arrived, so she swung through the kitchen door, overcome by hunger, and did not reappear in the lounge until close to cocktail hour.

"That dame's a weirdo." Johnny whistled as I came in to show him how to make the soupe de poisson we had on the menu. Johnny was a pre-med student at school and considered the kitchen his *surgery* and anyone who entered that sanctum his patient—open to diagnosis. "Did you look at her eyes? No pupils! Black as olives without pits. And she seldom blinks them! Try that sometime. It's damned near impossible. Twenty-minute stretches without blinking her eyes once!"

"What did she talk to you about?" I asked, alerted.

"You wouldn't believe it! She says she's a great niece of Eleanor and Franklin and they have the FBI and the CIA and all the local authorities follow her every move, and that they plan to kill her and make it look like suicide because she has secret information no other living person has about Franklin's reign. That's what she called it—*Franklin's Reign*. She's as nutty as Planter's peanuts!"

By the time I spoke to Steve about it, he had already been cornered by several guests, who talked about Rosamond's odd behavior, and by Cornelia and Nancy, who revealed that Rosamond's carpetbag contained a collection of small cakes of soap from dozens of inns, motels and hotels, but nothing else.

"Do you remember the names of any place advertised on the soap wrappers?" Steve asked Nancy.

"The Swan Inn in Old Chatham," Nancy recalled. "I

worked there the season before I got married."

Steve put in a call to the Swan Inn. "She just left here," the innkeeper advised us. "She's mentally ill, but her psychiatrist at the institute told me he thought she was quite harmless. They sent someone over to take her back but by then she was gone."

"Did she pay her bill?" Steve asked.

"Steve!" I cried on the extension. "Who cares? Ask him for the name of the institute and the psychiatrist!"

Rosamond turned out to be a rich girl who had lost her entire family in a plane crash and had suffered a mental breakdown, believing that the family had been murdered in a plot and that there was also a plot to kill her. She was, of course, no relation to Franklin and Eleanor.

She recognized the two men who came to take her back to the institute and hid behind me, whispering fiercely in my ear, "Don't let them take me. They're agents sent to assassinate me because I'm a Roosevelt!"

The incident left Steve and me troubled. One cannot remain untouched by such sadness. Furthermore, though there are many "Rosamond Roosevelts" in this world, one does not open one's home to them. As innkeepers we had no choice. The terrified eyes of the distracted girl haunted me for weeks.

Paul arrived for his yearly audit. This time everything was neatly set out for him, thanks to Cornelia's efficiency. All this seemed to do, however, was make the bad news come quicker. "I don't know how you've managed it," he told us later that same day over a long Scotch which didn't seem to help his short temper, "but this year you've lost *seventeen thousand three hundred and forty-six dollars and seventy eight cents!* That's an increase . . ."

"Never mind the statistics," Steve interrupted.

"What do you mean 'Never mind the statistics'? You'll have to pay back those loans," he warned.

"They weren't actually loans," Steve explained. "We put in monies from my teaching and from Anne's writing."

"You did what?" Paul's hand shook as he put down his glass. "No one ever invests his own money in a poor-risk business like a restaurant-inn!"

"Yeah—well, we did, Paul, and that shows you the faith we have. It just happened to be *one of those years*. Hell, we got hit with a gas shortage, inflation and bad weather," Steve protested.

"What makes you think next year it won't be locusts and fire?" Paul demanded.

"Look at the place," I tried to reason with him. "Isn't it really beautiful now? Did you see the third floor? They're the favorite rooms and only last year they were the attic dormitory. And our suite and the upstairs terrace . . ."

"Don't remind me of that," he wailed. "You'll never recoup those expenses. How about the twenty-five percent rule? You've raised your prices fifteen percent and your expenses have gone up twenty. You're in even worse shape than you were last year."

"Don't be such a pessimist," Steve argued. "We took in much more money in less time. We're well known now. We've had national publicity and finally wooed the locals. We're in all the tour books and even received a request from *Gourmet* magazine for one of our recipes."

"I keep telling you, all I know is what I see on the bottom line, and that's in bright red and taking up five columns! I'd feel a helluva lot better if *Gourmet* magazine wanted to pay you for that recipe!"

"Okay, Paul, the books are in bad shape, but the inn looks great and the season facing us can be fantastic," I began.

"*Will be* fantastic," Steve amended.

"What can we do to get the most out of it?" I asked.

"Raise your prices and lower your costs for a start," Paul advised, "and begin to look at the place as a business, not a theatrical enterprise, and an inn, not a home."

I saw the pain in Steve's face and I reached for his hand. "We'll make it work, Paul," I said quietly, my eyes on Steve, "but it has to work Steve's way."

By the time Paul left, he was even more displeased because we told him we planned to buy an extra ice machine, turn the area off the back kitchen into a walk-in refrigerated room and to purchase dessert and hors d'oeuvre carts like the ones we had seen in Paris.

For several days after Paul's departure Steve walked sadly around the inn. I would see him pacing his property, pausing by the graceful poplar border, by the patch of lush firs, hands thrust deep into his pockets. The inn, the five acres, those trees and the view of the lavender hills all had deep meaning to him. Orpheus had been a dream. I understood that. It was to have been something *he* created, an extension of himself. If Orpheus was failing it gave him a personal sense of failure, too.

We hit upon the idea to add a private bathroom to Lex's room, redo it and to move out of the inn for the season. We would rent our "home" in order to bring in more revenue, to fit in two more couples who would eat and drink at our new 25 percent increase in prices. It was not an easy decision. It meant packing all our personal possessions away and it seemed at first that it would leave us without roots for the summer.

We leased two large old rooms in a nearby hotel for a small percentage of what we could rent our own. The move would give us privacy and a place to escape the tensions that living at the inn during season involved.

It is difficult even now to evaluate our emotions about the inn during that terrible Watergate summer. Guests spent long hours bent over the television set in the sitting room. There were heated discussions by the pool, despair on La Verandah, disgust at the bar and indigestion in the restaurant. It was a summer of discontent, a season of disillusionment, and it seemed to take more to buoy our guests' spirits and give them a sense of luxe and comfort, of surcease from the nation's woes.

It was not only Paul or Watergate that gave us a sense of the dire state of affairs at the inn and in the country. We were, for one thing, at the mercy of the telephone in our hotel room, always on call, no matter what the hour of the day or night— we were "inn doctors," listening to all the aches, pains and complications; we received hourly bulletins, diagnosing and finally having to interrupt our private life to run over to the inn to deal with the emergencies firsthand.

Also, since we had no room at the inn for our own use, there was no place during a long, hot day or an equally long, hot, exhausting night to collapse for ten or fifteen minutes. We often had to remain at the inn for stretches of ten to twelve hours, and there was no private bathroom or shower or terrace.

That year, on my birthday, Richard Nixon left office in disgrace. Every guest at the inn felt as if a member of his own family had let him personally down. Halfway through that evening, Steve grabbed me by the arm and insisted we leave and have our own "birthday celebration." We never had left Orpheus unmanned during peak hours, but Yousef was on and there wasn't a full house, so off we went.

Steve had bought me a marvelous, slinky sky-blue jersey ensemble—gown, jacket and mile-long scarf. I looked a bit like Isadora Duncan dressed as Rita Hayworth—or perhaps it was the other way around. I felt sensational, but the outfit presented a small social problem. Guests could wear denims with diamonds at Orpheus and often did, but in this ensemble I would have been out of place at the Red Lion Inn, for example. We decided on an inn about forty miles away which was supposed to be our nearest competition in elegance and style. (Paul had also reminded us that he knew *they* were in the black because he was friendly with their accountant.)

It was called the Belgian Arms and it sat like a fat red rooster at a junction of two main roads, its red-brick façade laced with

160

English ivy. It was not a restaurant I could sweep into, jersey gown clinging to my body, scarf flying in the summer breezes. The mood was set as you crossed the threshold. Monsieur Le Gant greeted us with a smile that strained itself through his admirable gleaming white teeth, flicked the edge of his neatly clipped mustache, raised a hairy gray eyebrow at my costume and asked Steve, "You 'ave a reservation?"

"Citron: two," Steve replied.

The *patron* snapped his fingers and miraculously a tuxedoed waiter appeared, bowed and led the way to a small table cut off from the main dining room by the service el. Steve wanted another table but I assured him I rather liked the privacy and the fantastic view of the kitchen activity.

There was no way you could confuse the identity of Madame Le Gant—primly dressed, pale and yet quite clearly possessing an iron will. She inspected every tray that came out of the kitchen, and recomputed each check the waiters brought her for final approval. Never did she step more than three feet from the kitchen. Muffled commands floated our way along with the delicious aromas.

"I bet she never fraternizes with the guests," I whispered.

"Hell," Steve replied, "I bet she doesn't even fraternize with Monsieur Le Gant!"

The food was good, served elegantly, and the prices were outrageous.

"How many rooms do they have upstairs?" I asked.

"Eight. Shall I book one for after dinner?" Steve leered, his hand slipping onto my knee.

"Don't be ridiculous. I mean, Paul says their bottom line is always in the black and they only have eight rooms—really the same number we have when we're in residence. Do you think they're doing something right or that we're doing something wrong?"

He sat there studying me. "I'm not sure," he said quietly. "But you know it's not like me to be early for a reservation.

Normally, I would insist we have a glass of champagne to celebrate your birthday at our own bar. But there was something that happened that made me want to leave Orpheus right away."

"What was it?" I asked.

"While you were dressing I went around to the tables checking everything, and there were these four young punks, maybe nineteen or twenty years old, from Pittsfield. Maybe you noticed them on our way out? They were seated at the banquette. They seemed to be enjoying their dinner, and I went over and asked if there was anything they needed. One of the kids looked up at me, grinning self-importantly. 'No,' he said, and grabbing my hand, he turned it palm upward and squashed something into it. 'But I won't need this,' he sneered, and then turned away. I looked down into my hand and there was a maraschino cherry, fish flakes clinging to it. Johnny had obviously thought he was being artistic and had put a cherry on this kid's sole Véronique. That snippy kid wanted me to know that cherries did not go with fish and that he was some kind of gourmet. Anyway, I stood there with this lousy cherry in my palm wanting to squash it in the punk kid's face, but I controlled myself and walked away—and then I did the damnedest thing."

"What?" I asked, my heart breaking.

"I swallowed it, and as I did I thought of all the unwanted things the two of us have had to swallow. The people we've been forced to welcome into our *home.*"

"Some of them have turned into real friends. Most of them have been very nice."

"There have been far too many rude and hostile guests. We don't draw a salary. We don't get unemployment or Social Security. We just put all our money in so that we can eat crow. What kind of life is that?"

"It won't always be like that," I rationalized. "You know you told Paul it would take five years. You expected that."

"Yes, and that didn't matter three years ago because my home life in New York was so much in the red. But now, with our life together such a plus, with having our children with us as we do . . ." He took my hand across the table. "It may seem corny, but I really dug last Thanksgiving when we had the inn as a home and Thanksgiving was a family holiday. I was terribly resentful of all the *invaders* in our house at Christmas and New Year's Eve. Here I am, a musician, and I haven't even been able to hear one Tanglewood concert this summer. And it seems a shame," he rushed on, "that we can't get more joy out of our life. The pressures of running the inn seem to be taking all the fun out of it. And I don't seem to need the adulation from outsiders anymore. I don't need to feed people, or teach them what good pop music is. In fact, I even resent the boors sleeping in our bedrooms with the elegant French toile fabrics on the walls."

"But you know most of them appreciate the uniqueness of Orpheus. It's rare that we get the cherry-handing type."

"I know. But I also know the type I am—and the type you are. Can you think of having your arms in dishwater forever when an employee doesn't show? Or me constantly nursing an ailing oil burner? Look at Madame Le Gant there. Do you see those lines in her face? They come from looking down at the checks and adding them up in the atmospheric light. In spite of her sour puss she's happy in that job. She's a born innkeeper. And Monsieur—he's delighted to scream or snap his fingers at the waiters, and I'm sure he has no loyalty to his staff. That's not me, and not you. Why, if Mrs. Gretchner hadn't left to marry Ronald, I would have kept her on until she was doing her duties in a wheelchair!"

"What are you trying to say?" I asked, knowing really, but needing him to speak the words.

"What I'm trying to say, darling, is that anyone *can't* run an inn. You have to be of a certain temperament. And that's why we do things 'wrong.' "

We sat there silently, waiting for the check, watching Madame Le Gant retotal it. And as we made our way to the front door, I caught a glimpse of Monsieur Le Gant, snapping his fingers for the waiter to ready our table for the next diners.

When I first came to live at the inn, I found it difficult to inquire what people did for a living or whether they were married or divorced. But I had overcome the feeling that it was faintly ill-mannered to ask biographical data of a guest. Now I knew most guests expected me to take the first step to give them a peg on which to hang a weekend's conversation.

Our guests for the big foliage weekend were a varied group and, for the most part, lively and interesting. With Tillie Goldman, a student of Steve's, as catalyst, an unusual intimacy immediately developed among the guests. Tillie loved people, loved finding out about them and putting them together. In a short time, she knew almost everyone's history, including a few secrets, and had drawn some cogent conclusions: the couple in Room 6 were *not* married; the couple in Room 8 who said they were *not* married, *were* ("At least twenty years," Tillie speculated—"They think this illicit charade will stimulate their libido"); Marian, the attractive young laboratory technician, had used most of her savings for the weekend hoping to meet an unattached man; Arthur, the handsome white-haired man with the Byronic nose, in the room next to hers, was a homosexual ("Charming though," Tillie sighed, "and a great sense of humor. He once sent a letter addressing Talullah as 'Dear Sir,' proposing marriage. You have to like a man like *that!*").

"But what," she asked, "have you found out about Guido Bernstein?"

She was referring to a young man who had taken the last available room—the windowless single—without a reservation. He had frequented the bar several times during the summer, always sitting alone—the cool, attractive observer. Though we knew nothing about him, he was not a stranger. "Well, he's neither Italian nor Jewish," I replied, recalling his lean, blond Nordic good looks.

"I think he's a hustler," Tillie confided. "At least he seems to be using a professional approach to seducing Marian, Arthur *and* the lady who says she's not married to her husband."

"He told Steve he was a theatrical producer, and that he had rented a place up here last summer when he used to come in, and that he had come back because he had thought some of the kids who perform here on the weekends had great potential," I offered.

"I think he's on the skids and it makes me a little nervous the way he keeps glancing at my hands," Tillie confessed. "In fact, I intended to ask you if you might take my jewelry and lock it up somewhere."

"But we haven't a safe," I replied.

"How about the freezer?" she suggested.

Tillie had brought some rather spectacular jewelry with her and so with great concern I spoke to Steve about the situation.

"Tillie's nervous about Guido," I began.

Steve closed our door tightly and spoke in a soft voice. "I'm nervous, too," he confessed. "Nancy says he has an axe in his room."

"There has to be some explanation," I stammered. "No one just travels around with an axe like it was a tennis racket."

We exchanged frightened looks.

"Forgive me, darling," Steve laughed uneasily. "I'm really flipping, I think! The summer was just too damned much work and I'm resenting not having our home to ourselves." He crossed back to the door. "He's down in the bar. I'm going to ask that kid what he's doing with an axe."

"Not alone you're not." I said, following him out of the room.

Guido told us, with an easy smile and a nonchalant manner, that he cut logs for exercise the way some men jogged. He said

165

he often went out into the woods and "swung the axe" for a half-hour or more. He claimed it kept him in shape.

Steve replied that we had to have his room and that he would have to settle his bill and leave. Marian was now clinging to his arm.

"That's all right." He grinned. "I'll move in with Marian for the night."

"Annie," Steve said hours later, when we were finally alone, "I have the responsibility of your safety and that of my guests in my hands and I have terrible doubts about Guido's sanity. He's not like Rosamond. She was a pathetic, distracted creature, but I never had any qualms about her endangering anyone's life. I'm no psychiatrist, but I don't like that guy's *look*. I don't know how I let him persuade me to rent him that room in the first place!"

"Did you originally say no?"

"Without faltering. But he had found out the room wasn't booked. And he became—what can I say—ingratiating, I guess. He loved Orpheus, admired me, thought the kids who appeared here were great—and he would pay in advance."

"Did he?"

"With a check. But, of course, it's Friday night, and there's no way to call the bank. I just thought he might be a fourflusher —and the room *was* empty. Damn it!" Steve said angrily. "I had no right to take *any* chance."

"Look, darling," I said, a cold terror suddenly overtaking me. "Do you think he's really endangering anyone's life?"

"I went through his briefcase when he was downstairs with Marian . . ."

"And?" I prodded.

"There was an appointment card with a psychiatrist in the same town as the bank branch he wrote the check on and I reached the man at his home. He was visibly taken aback that Guido—his real name is Sven Larsen—was here and that he had an axe with him. Guido had an appointment with the

166

doctor this morning but never showed up. He has a psychotic history. Just before he came here he had axed his father's German shepherd."

I flinched and Steve took my hands and held them tightly in his. "His mother finally convinced her husband to seek private help for him. Guido promised to cooperate but managed to break out of the house and come here—I think because it felt warm and welcoming when he was in Stockbridge this summer."

"Why was he here in the first place?"

"I asked the psychiatrist the same question. He said that Sven really wanted help but was terrified of what he might discover about himself, and that perhaps being so close to Austin Riggs, the psychiatric hospital, he thought he might get some inadvertent help."

"Okay, darling," I said weakly. "What do we do?"

"We can't call the police because he hasn't done anything. He hasn't even threatened us. And it's too late for anything drastic tonight. What I thought we could do, if you agree, is to turn off the heat and tell everyone in the morning that the furnace has broken down and we can't get it repaired before Monday and that they will have to leave."

"Paul will never approve." I smiled nervously.

"Do you?"

"One hundred percent."

Neither of us took more than a cat nap that night, keeping our door ajar so that we could hear any sound of movement in the inn. In the middle of the night we heard Guido's door open. Steve had remained fully dressed and quickly got up. I wrapped a blanket around me and followed him to the door. The house was freezing and I was shivering. Steve motioned for me to return to bed but I was not about to leave him standing there in the hallway alone. I grasped his arm and held on tightly as he edged his way noiselessly into the corridor, gripping the old reliable fire poker in one hand.

167

Both of us could see Guido's large shadowy figure proceed down the hall to Marian's room. There was no axe in his hand. He tried the door and then entered. We stood there not quite knowing what to do, but in less than five minutes he was back in the hallway again. We watched frozen and silent as he returned to his own room and closed the door.

Everyone awoke early, as the inn was like an arctic zone. "What's happened to the heat?" the guests wanted to know.

"The furnace broke down. We've been up all night trying to nurse it, but it's absolutely kaput," Steve lied. "We've called Joe, the plumber, but he can't get the right parts until Monday. I'm afraid you'll all have to go elsewhere."

Guido was still there when everyone else had left. Steve and I sat huddled before the living room fire waiting for him to come downstairs. He stood smiling coldly in the doorway.

"Would you like me to see if I can fix the furnace?" he asked.

"No. We'd like you to leave, Guido, because we're locking up and going to the Red Lion Inn ourselves," Steve replied.

Guido shrugged his shoulders and went out of the room. We heard him in the bar telephoning someone but decided not to investigate. It seemed an eternity, but finally the bar door swung shut and there was the sound of his car as he drove down the driveway. We immediately ran into the bar and locked the door.

"The ten-dollar bill over the bar . . ." Steve cried, pointing to the spot where the first money taken by Orpheus had been scotch-taped to the mirror. "He took it."

He had left the axe resting on the pillow of his bed. It was weird. Steve rang Chief Obie and he agreed to have the inn patrolled, but we spent a terrible twenty-four hours until we heard that Guido had made that last call to Austin Riggs. They had told him to come to them, at which point they had contacted his family and the psychiatrist Steve had spoken to.

168

"We're going to sell Orpheus," Steve said as soon as he was off the telephone.

"You're sure this is what you want to do?" I asked.

"I've been considering it since the end of summer, as you know. I had some doubts then—but none, whatsoever, now."

I sat in the deserted lounge while he played the piano long into the night, stage lights glaring, sound system up to the highest decibel. Finally he rose from the piano, and smiling as he leaned down, kissed me on the forehead. "It's not so painful," he whispered, "when you don't have to face it alone." "Look at the dividend I got." And then we sleepily turned out the lights and went up to bed.

PART

FIVE

Once the decision had been made, I wasted no time. I called Stef and asked her to handle the sale. After we discussed a fair asking price, the contents of the ad and its placement, I added, "They have to be special people. I don't want Orpheus turned into a hamburger joint." I knew she understood, for she had the same love for her own inn that we had for Orpheus.

For six weeks Stef ran an ad in *The New York Times*, but there was very little response. With the economy as it was, it looked as if selling the inn was not going to be an easy task. Anne and I went more frequently to New York now, staying several days at a time. Perhaps we stayed away so much because we could not bear to see Orpheus in a state of limbo, waiting around for anyone who would have it. Also, the oil burner was working so fitfully that we were most often chilled to the bone. We would make roaring fires, roasting on one side and freezing on the other. We talked much of the future, of Anne's writing, my music and what our life together was going to be in New York. I had grandiose plans for enlarging the studio, teaching only professionals and adding courses in drama and movement. She talked excitedly of a new sweeping historical novel she planned.

Early one morning Stef called. "Stephen, could I bring over a couple to see the inn? They want to see it right away. They just drove up from New York and they're very interested in finding a business in the Berkshires." Then she whispered into the mouthpiece, "I think they have money."

Anne and I scurried around trying to get the rooms in order. I pushed the thermostat up, hoping the oil burner would respond. A click, a whine and then nothing. I figured we'd tell them that the burner needed repair, and if we went to closing I would take the $3,000 cost of replacing it off the purchase price. Meanwhile, I added more wood to our already blazing fires and turned on the ovens in the kitchen to help warm the rear of the house.

Stef smiled expansively as she introduced us.

"It's freezing in here," Mrs. Williams exclaimed. "Harold, I wouldn't remove my coat if I were you."

"Well, of course," Stef interrupted, charm oozing from her lips, "Stephen has plans to put in a new heater. It will keep the place beautifully warm and be more economical." She added quickly, "But did you ever see such a marvelous fireplace? Imagine how glorious it would be to dine beside it when the snow is thick. That fireplace would be absolutely divine reflected in a goblet of ruby Châteauneuf-du-Pape. Don't you think so, Mrs. Williams?"

Mrs. Williams, her harsh, thin face set in an expression of disbelief, quite frankly did not know how to reply.

"What does your fuel bill run per month?" Mr. Williams asked.

"Mrs. Barber has all the figures in the prospectus. With the new furnace you can expect the fuel bill to be less than half. But we can go over all the details once you've seen the inn," I said, hedging, knowing that three years of constant losses would bode ill to a man whose major concern was the fuel bill. "Stephanie, I am sure Mr. and Mrs. Williams would like to see the kitchen, and then you might take them upstairs."

Stephanie gave me an arch look, swung her long black cloak over one shoulder so that only the tips of her Cossack boots were exposed, pulled her huge fur hat down tightly over her ears and led them away. I stood grasping Anne's hand, unable to follow.

"I don't like them much," I said to her.

"You probably wouldn't like anyone who was going to take over Orpheus. Frankly, I don't feel anything for them either. But they have a beady directness that will probably make them as successful as the Le Gants."

"Maybe you're right," I said.

I left the room and caught up with them in the kitchen. They examined every escargot dish and stockpot. They peered into every cupboard, and Mr. Williams tried the gas jets on our beautiful Garland range to see if it was in good repair. Then we went outside and walked every inch of the ground. It was freezing and I was aware that Mrs. Williams could hardly catch her breath. I suggested tea inside. Mr. Williams rejected the offer, preferring to remain outside to examine the foundation, but Mrs. Williams quickly accepted and made her way back to the house.

Once inside I showed her our splendid reviews. She read them silently, pausing from time to time to look around at the lounge and to peer into the bar. Poor Stef had remained outside. As I glanced out the window I saw Mr. Williams push her ungallantly to one side and make a rush for the bar door.

"Mr. Citron," he said breathlessly, grabbing me by the arm, "follow me." He dragged me out around the front of the house, pushing me down to look beneath La Verandah.

"See that?" he exclaimed.

"What?" I asked, not able to see a thing in the narrow crawlspace.

"Porcupine," he replied in a horror-filled voice.

"Porcupine?" I asked, crawling back out and having trouble straightening.

"They are gnawing away at your struts. They might ruin the foundation. The inn could collapse, you know?" he intoned. "The foundation has a big crack over by the bar anyway."

"The building has been standing here for nearly a hundred and thirty years. I don't think you have any worry about its falling down now," I said, but I could see he was not mollified.

He shook his shaggy-dog face and said, "The place is in imminent danger. I would have to have an expert look at it before I make any firm offer."

"As you like," I said quickly, my dislike for the man growing with every gust of wind that swept around the corner of the house. "But I'm sure Mrs. Barber has told you that someone else is extremely interested and already discussing it with his lawyers."

Stef's eyes opened wide but she remained silent. I was not so sure she hadn't frozen for that matter! But Mr. Williams merely smiled rather snidely.

"Your asking price is out of line, of course," he said, "in view of all that has to be done."

"What *all?*"

"Why, we would have to start from scratch. I would take down all that fabric from the walls and put up Sanitas. It stays much cleaner, and you never have to worry about kids scrawling with crayons on the wall."

"Except for my own son, children under ten are not permitted at the inn," I informed him.

"You cut out all the family business," he said, shaking his head.

"We keep open late. We're a supper club after all, and the menu is quite sophisticated—escargots and crêpes. Not right for most children," I explained.

"That's another thing. We would have to change the menu entirely. New England inns should serve New England cooking," he said axiomatically.

"Wouldn't you be throwing away all the good will Stephen has created over these three years, Mr. Williams?" Stef asked. Then picking up her cold feet stiffly one at a time, she added,

176

"Perhaps if we go inside and you have one of Stephen's home-made croissants you'll change your mind."

When we returned to the lounge I could hear that Anne was having her own problems with Mrs. Williams.

"The place would have to be completely relit. Probably rewired. We would want TV in all the rooms and air conditioning for the summer season," Mrs. Williams was saying.

"Air conditioning is not really necessary. You know, we are on the highest elevation in Stockbridge," Anne said, trying to be polite. "And people shouldn't come to the country to watch TV in an air-conditioned room."

"Everything stays cleaner with air acclimitization," Mrs. Williams informed us.

Mr. Williams sat down on the banquette beside her, helped himself to a croissant and took one bite. "Butter," he gasped, as though he had just been poisoned.

"You know, Harold, I was thinking we could make accommodations for ourselves here on the ground floor. We would just have to divide the gallery in half, put up a ceiling to cover those exposed beams and attach some plumbing in the back closet."

A numbing thought came to me. Mr. and Mrs. Williams were bound to undo everything I had tried to achieve. Stef, a good businesswoman, gave me a withering look as I started to speak, and I held my tongue.

"That's just the way it was when Stephen found the place, and it would cost very little to make your own quarters on the ground floor." She thrust a ring-covered hand through the slit in her cloak and dramatically lifted a croissant to her orange lips. "Oh my! These are so good they *must* be sinful, Stephen," she said.

"Now that we've seen the state of the house," Mr. Williams said, rising, "let's go inside to the office and you'll show me the p. and l. statements and the journals."

As I led the way to the office, Mrs. Williams confided, "Harold can't eat anything rich. Gall bladder. It's all a part of the success syndrome, I suppose."

Reluctantly, I showed Mr. Williams the profit and loss statements and opened all the books that Paul and Cornelia had kept so marvelously up to date. But no matter how neat the ledgers looked, you could not ignore the fact that the inn had been operating at tremendous losses for over three years.

Harold examined every column and made pages of notes, spending nearly an hour in the process. Frequently he would excuse himself and join Mrs. Williams for a brief whispered conversation. Feeling *de trop*, I went into the lounge with Anne and Stef while Mrs. Williams roamed the upstairs.

"No, Stef," I practically snarled. "Not the Williamses. It simply is not possible."

Before she could reply both Mr. and Mrs. Williams came into the room, and standing in army at-ease positions, announced that in spite of everything having to be redone and the shocking losses indicated in the books, they were prepared to make an offer.

Both Stef and Anne stared at me as I stepped brashly forward and announced, "I can't accept *any* offer. I just received a telephone call from the other people who I told you were interested." I spouted my lie rapidly, afraid that if I stopped talking I would weaken. "They've just put a binder on the place and gave a deposit check to our lawyer. Of course if you want second option? They're paying the full price, though, and they want to have a closing very soon."

Stephanie interjected, "I'm *desolé*, really I am, but"—she grinned and put her arm through Harold's—"I have another inn over in Richmond that you might be interested in. Since you're up here, why don't we drive over and see it." She turned to me. "I'll call you later, *mon cheri*," she cooed and swept them out. "Now, Richmond," I heard her say, "there's a place that would need no work. Very modern. Used to be a motel that they converted into an inn."

Mr. Williams came back to shake my hand. "I'd check those porcupines right away if I were you," he said.

It was over three weeks before Stef called to say she had another interested "looker." We were deep into November and the first heavy snow had begun to fall. I saw a woman get out of Stef's steadfast Renault and then pause rather dramatically in the driveway, the thick flakes of snow falling on her bare, dark head. Stef took her by the elbow and brought her inside.

"Stephen, this is Rosemary Taylor," Stef introduced.

"Rosie. Everyone calls me Rosie." She grabbed my hand and shook it. She was a large woman, dressed in smart tweeds, with a warm, strong voice. Her eyes were wide and brown and she looked straight at you.

As I led the way into the breakfast room she said, "Exactly how I imagined it would be!"

"Rosie has wanted an inn for a long time," Stef explained. "I don't know why I didn't think of advertising in the *Berkshire Eagle* as well as *The New York Times.* You know, we never think of people who *live* in the country wanting to have a country inn. But here's living proof that they have the same dreams we fugitives from the cities have."

"I've passed Orpheus so many times," Rosemary said, "but I never came up the driveway before."

Anne came into the room and I introduced her to Rosie.

"How come you never came up the driveway?" I asked.

"Well, I haven't gone *anywhere* these last couple of years. I was in the process of getting a divorce and life was quite complicated." She turned to Anne. "Well, you know . . ."

"We know," we all answered together.

"Can we start with the kitchen?" Rosie asked.

179

We did an about-face and reentered the lounge. Rosie stopped in the doorway, took a deep breath and said, "Why, Mr. Citron, you've done a fantastic job, it's a beautiful room, it has such a warm provençal feeling. And what a perfect place for the piano!"

"Call me Steve," I said. "As for the piano, that placement was Anne's idea."

"The whole room looks like it was done with love."

"It was," Stef said.

"Living proof," she added as she noticed Anne and me holding hands.

Rosie fell in love with the Garland stove, rhapsodized about the walk-in cold room and exchanged menu ideas and recipes. "Taylor is my husband's name. I'm Italian. Piedmontese, in fact. What I like to cook is not that far from your recipes. We both believe in butter, I know."

"And undercooked fresh vegetables," I added.

We walked out onto La Verandah. "How lovely." She smiled, and then added, as the November wind whipped around the corner, "Perhaps it could be glassed in. Then it could be used year-round. I've often seen the people dining out here in the summer. I'm sure they would love it even more in the autumn or with the winter snow at their feet. I mean, look at that view. You could travel all over Europe and not find anything more lovely."

"You know, that's exactly what Steve and I were hoping to do next spring," Anne confessed. "Glass in La Verandah, using sliding windows that can be pushed back in summer."

"I'd use doors, floor to ceiling, not windows," Rosie said. "I wouldn't want to lose an inch of that view."

"Shall we go upstairs?" Stef asked, smiling broadly.

As Rosie went to pass me she took my hand tightly in hers. "You have to understand," she said seriously, "I've always loved cooking for people and entertaining. I think of myself as kind of a professional hostess. And it's always been my dream

. . . yes, I think always . . . that someday I would own an inn."
And she swept up the front staircase.

Within a month the transfer of title was completed and the
inn was hers. We had found a large old apartment in New York
and were packed and ready to move. It was a week before
Christmas and the row of fir trees to the left of the entrance
sign were frosted with ice. There was a clear December sun
shimmering on the snow-banked roof.

"Oh migosh," I said to Anne, who sat beside me as we
started down the driveway for the last time. "I hope the
kitchen ceiling isn't going to leak when that snow melts."

Anne smiled softly and said, "Well, that's no longer our
concern."

"I know," I said, "it's Rosie's now."

We turned down Route 7. I watched Orpheus in the rear-
view mirror until we rounded the bend. Then it was gone. For
a moment I thought I would have to turn back.

"How about taking a chunk of our sale profit and flying to
France?" Anne asked.

I gripped her hand. "While we're there," I said, "maybe we
could look at villas on the Côte d'Azur. I've always had the idea
of opening a music camp for Americans who want to learn
French and music. What if we could find a place overlooking
the Mediterranean, and . . ."

ABOUT THE AUTHORS

ANNE EDWARDS is the author of five previous novels,
including *Child of Night, The Hesitant Heart,
Haunted Summer,* and the best-selling *The Survivors.*
She has also written *Judy Garland: A Biography*
and has worked on numerous film scripts.
She is currently writing a biography of Vivien Leigh.

STEPHEN CITRON is a pianist and music teacher,
whose studios are at Carnegie Hall in New York City.
He is currently at work on a book
about the French cabaret called *Les Cabarets.*

Ms. Edwards and Mr. Citron are now living happily in
New York City.